DATE DUE			

CZECH REPUBLIC

Efstathia Sioras

MARSHALL CAVENDISH
New York • London • Sydney

Reference edition reprinted 2000 by
Marshall Cavendish Corporation
99 White Plains Road
Tarrytown
New York 10591

© Times Media Private Limited 1999

Originated and designed by
Times Books International, an imprint of
Times Media Private Limited, a member of the
Times Publishing Group

Printed in Malaysia

Library of Congress Cataloging-in-Publication Data:
Sioras, Efstathia
     Czech Republic / Efstathia Sioras.
         p. cm.—(Cultures Of The World)
     Includes bibliographical references and index.
     Summary: Describes the geography, history, government,
economy, people, lifestyle, religion, language, arts, leisure,
festivals, and food of the Czech Republic.
     ISBN 0-7614-0870-3 (library binding)
     1. Czech Republic—Juvenile literature. [1. Czech
Republic.] I. Title. II. Series.
DB2065.S56   1999
943.71—dc21   98–30290
                        CIP
                        AC

INTRODUCTION

THE CZECH REPUBLIC came into existence on January 1, 1993. Although a new country, the history and culture of its people span more than a thousand years. Czech writers and composers have left their mark in the international arena. It is a country of contrasts, with forested hills and mountainsides surrounding lush lowlands. The cities and towns have striking architecture and the countryside is dotted with castles, spires, and resorts that speak evocatively of the republic's cultural heritage and wealth.

The Czech Republic is home to a people that have often been subject to foreign rule. They are people with a strong sense of cultural identity. In 1991, they rejected their communist rulers and demanded their right to self-determination. They continue to strive toward their ideal of a just society for all, despite the harsh realities of the modern capitalist world they have chosen.

CONTENTS

Standing guard with rifle in hand at one of the many castles in the Czech Republic.

CONTENTS

Admiring the view from one of the beautiful buildings in the Old Town, Prague.

GEOGRAPHY

THE CZECH REPUBLIC is situated in the heart of Europe. This landlocked country shares borders with Austria, Germany, Poland, and the Republic of Slovakia. It is slightly smaller than the state of South Carolina in the United States.

The country's geography is neatly divided between agricultural land and forests. Continuous forest belts can be found bordering the mountains, while the lowlands have traditionally been developed for agricultural needs. Although large areas of original forest have been cleared for cultivation and for timber, woodlands continue to remain a feature of the Czech landscape.

The republic's scenery varies dramatically, from limestone caves and natural springs to beautiful mountain ranges and numerous rivers. Cities and towns are well distributed throughout the land.

It is estimated that by the year 2000 air pollution will have destroyed 70% of the forests in the Czech Republic.

Opposite: **View of Prague from Charles Bridge, which links the two halves of the city.**

Left: **The rock mountain in Bohemia called "The Organ."**

A section of the Giant or Krkonoše Mountains in Bohemia.

BOHEMIA TO THE WEST

The Czech Republic consists of two major regions—Bohemia to the west and Moravia to the east. Their landscape differs, Bohemia being essentially a 1,640 feet (500 m) high plateau surrounded by low mountains while Moravia is mostly lowland.

Bohemia is drained by the Labe River (also called the Elbe River), which provides access to the North Sea. Its tributary, the Vltava (also called the Moldau), at 270 miles (435 km), is the longest river in the Czech Republic. The region's chief towns are Prague, Plzeň, and České Budějovice.

The mountains providing a natural border for Bohemia are the Šumava Mountains to the southwest, the Ore Mountains to the northwest, forming the border with Germany, the Krkonoše (Giant) Mountains along the

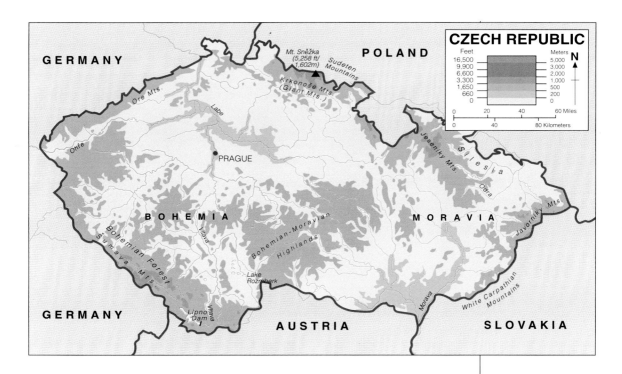

Polish border to the northeast, and the Bohemian-Moravian Highlands that divide Bohemia and Moravia. Mount Sněžka (5,258 feet/1,602 m) is the highest mountain in the republic and part of the Giant mountain range.

Bohemia is subdivided into five regions—North, South, East, West, and Central Bohemia. The topography of South Bohemia is unusual. Since the 16th century the land around the city of České Budějovice has been sculpted into a network of hundreds of linked fish ponds and artificial lakes. Today they are used to breed Bohemia's Christmas carp.

The republic's largest artificial lake is also located in the south, near Třeboň—Lake Rožmberk was created in 1590 and is about 1,235 acres (500 hectares). The republic's other large body of water is the Lipno Dam near the Austrian border.

North Bohemia has long been the most highly industrialized region of the Czech Republic. It is the site of extensive coal and iron-ore mining. As a result, its landscape resembles an eerie moonscape, while the burning of mainly low-quality brown coal causes severe air pollution.

Boating on a river in South Moravia.

MORAVIA TO THE EAST

Essentially lowland, Moravia is also surrounded by mountains: to the west the Bohemian-Moravian Highlands, to the east the White Carpathians and the Javorníky Mountains, and to the north the Jeseníky Mountains. Moravia's chief cities are Ostrava and Brno. Moravia is divided into North and South Moravia. In northeast Moravia there is also a historic region called Silesia. Silesia was a Polish province that was passed to Bohemia in 1335 and taken by Prussia in 1742. Most of Silesia was returned to Poland in 1945; the rest forms part of Germany and the Czech Republic.

Two main rivers in this region are the Morava River, which flows south to the Danube and eventually drains into the Black Sea, and the Odra (also called Oder) River, which swings around the eastern end of the Sudeten range into Poland and drains into the Baltic Sea. The Odra River caused extensive flooding in mid-1997—the worst since record keeping began in the early 19th century. A third of the republic was flooded for 10 days, over 40 people died, 2,500 were injured, and 10,000 made homeless. Due to the devastation of agricultural land, the republic had to import 440,800 tons (400,000 metric tonnes) of grain to prevent a food shortage.

In the southwest, just north of the city of Brno, is the wooded highland area called the Moravian Karst where limestone hills have been carved into canyons and hundreds of caves. Over millions of years, mildly acidic rainwater has seeped through the limestone rock, slowly dissolving sections of it. This has resulted in cave formations filled with colored stalactites and stalagmites.

The hills of South Moravia are renowned for their wineries, which export some excellent wines. This area also produces some fiery plum and apricot brandies, which are favorites of the Czechs.

RIVERS

There are three principal river systems: the Labe, the Odra, and the Morava rivers and their tributaries. The country's rivers flow to three different seas: those in southern Moravia flow to the Danube and onward to the Black Sea, the Labe flows to the North Sea, and the Odra to the Baltic Sea. The journeys these rivers make are long: the Black Sea is 466 miles (750 km) to the southeast, the North Sea is 329 miles (530 km) to the northwest, and the Baltic Sea is 217 miles (350 km) to the north.

The Vltava River is the longest river in the Czech Republic. It flows north across Bohemia and drains into the Labe River 18 miles (29 km) north of Prague.

A VARIABLE CLIMATE

The Czech Republic has a humid, continental climate. There are four distinct seasons, including hot, wet summers and drier winters. Temperature and rainfall fluctuate widely due to variable air pressure, and the weather in the republic is known for its changeable nature.

In Moravia, there is wide variation in temperature between winter and summer, day and night. Bohemia receives the moderating influence of an oceanic climate, so day and night temperatures do not vary as much. There is higher precipitation and more cloudy weather here than in Moravia.

Skiers on the slopes of the Krkonoše (Giant) Mountains.

Average summer temperatures range between 55°F and 73°F (13–23°C). Lowland temperatures often rise above 86°F (30°C). July is the hottest month of the year. In the summer, it rains on average every other day, with hot spells usually broken by heavy thunderstorms. In the highlands, temperatures are generally cooler, as they fall with increasing elevation; the mountains often experience near freezing conditions.

Winter temperatures in the Czech Republic average between 25°F and 28°F (–4°C and –2°C), with January being the coldest month. Temperatures can drop to 5°F (–15°C) in the lowlands, while in the highlands surrounding the Bohemian plateau, where Prague is situated, it can be bitterly cold.

Snow and fog are typical in the lowlands, with 40 to 100 days of snow in the winter. There will typically be 130 days of snow in the mountains. The Czech Republic does not have a really dry season. The winter months are slightly drier, with precipitation an average of one day in three. Rainfall averages 20–30 inches (50–76 cm) annually in the lowlands and 32 inches (81 cm) or more in the highlands.

Autumn leaves near Český Krumlov.

The Czech Republic is located in the main European watershed. Many central European rivers originate here. The country's main source of fresh water is precipitation that forms rivers. Rivers are at their highest in the spring and at their lowest in the summer. There are also a few freshwater lakes. Most lakes, such as those in Southern Bohemia, have been artificially created and provide a source of fish for local consumption.

FLORA AND FAUNA

The Czech landscape, from agricultural lowlands to steppes and mountain ranges, supports a wide range of vegetation. Despite several hundred years of clear-cutting for cultivation and decades of unregulated industrial development, one-third of the republic is covered by forest. Deciduous trees such as oaks are found in the lower regions of Moravia. Spruce is typical in the lower mountain areas, with beech at higher elevations. Beech and spruce forests cover the mountains in the country. Dwarf pine is common near the tree line. Above the tree line (approximately 4,595 feet/1,400 meters) are only grasses, shrubs, and lichens.

The Czech Republic is rich in fauna. Agricultural activities have allowed certain species such as hamsters to thrive. Introduced species have spread rapidly, for example muskrats, pheasants, and trout. A rich variety of wildlife inhabits lower areas of the mountains: bears (almost extinct now), wolves, lynx, foxes, wildcats, marmots, otters, marten, deer, and mink. The chamois, a mountain antelope hunted for its beautiful coat, came dangerously close to extinction. It is now protected and its numbers are increasing.

Hunted wildlife common to the woodlands and marshes are hares, rabbits, hamsters, gophers, partridge, pheasant, ducks, and wild geese. Protected species include the large birds—golden eagles, vultures, ospreys, storks, bustards, eagle-owls, and capercaillies (large grouse).

The country's national parks include the Bohemian Forest and the Krkonoše Mountains. The Bohemian Forest is part of an eco-tourism project shared by the Czech Republic, Austria, and Bavaria in Germany. This hopes to develop the tourism industry in an environmentally friendly way, preserving the beautiful landscape and historical sites. Many local people, however, do not favor the project, seeing it only as a plan to resettle them away from modern conveniences.

Opposite: **Trees in the Bohemian Forest in West Moravia. Some of the trees in Boubínský Prales Forest, which is a conservation area in the Bohemian Forest, are 400 years old. Much of the fauna and rare flora of the region attracts botanists and zoologists.**

CITIES

Over hundreds of years, towns in the region of the Czech Republic developed in a dense network of settlements, many just a few miles from each other. Today, they number approximately 15,300. Development was irregular and has typically resulted in small towns of fewer than 5,000 inhabitants. Classified as rural settlements, they total 98% of all settlements. With a population of approximately 10.3 million, there are 339 persons per square mile (131 persons per square km). By comparison, the average density in the United States is about 11 persons per square mile (28 persons per square km). Over 70% of Czechs live in urban areas. The greatest density is to be found in industrial areas such as North Bohemia, the lowest density along the border in South Bohemia.

Prior to the industrial revolution, Czechs cultivated the land they lived on. With industrialization, urban areas burgeoned and changed the Czechs' relationship with the land. This has generally resulted in environmental degradation, crowding, and a decline in the quality of life.

Due to the deterioration of the quality of life in urban areas many Czechs purchased holiday homes in the less affected countryside. Farms and old village houses were bought, restored, and renovated. This trend has saved much rural architecture that would otherwise have fallen to ruins. Unfortunately, the construction of new holiday homes has also damaged valuable agricultural land in some areas.

The government has responded to the concern of Czechs over the adverse effects on the environment of unregulated industrial development and urban sprawl by curtailing further extensive growth of towns and villages at the expense of agricultural land and forests. It has also been encouraging greater density in existing urban areas and the redevelopment of derelict inner city areas. In 1996 the Czech Republic Forest Act came into force. It is the first of such laws to deal comprehensively with forest management and contains restrictions designed to reinforce the effective conservation of forests.

PRAGUE A legend about Prague tells of a princess of a Slav tribe known as the Czechs, named after the leader of the tribe. This princess stood upon a high rock above a river and uttered the following prophecy: "I see a city whose splendor shall reach the stars." The princess was named Libuše, the river was the Vltava, and the city became Prague.

Prague is at the geographical center of Central Bohemia. It has been at the heart of Czech history since the Great Bohemian empire in the 9th century. The republic's longest river, the Vltava, flows through the city.

The Old Town Hall clock designed by Nikolaus von Kaaden stands in the Old Town Square of Prague. Constructed in 1410, it has two clockfaces; the lower one is a calendar that moves one day when the clock above strikes midnight.

16

Affectionately named "the city of 100 spires," Prague displays Romanesque, Gothic, Renaissance, Baroque, and Art Nouveau styles of architecture. Several bridges link the west and east banks of the Vltava, but its landmark bridge is Charles Bridge, a stone bridge begun in 1357 and lined with sculptures, the earliest placed in 1683, the most recent in 1928.

Prague is organized into several historical districts. On the west bank is the castle district of Hradčany with its 1,100-year-old castle and the magnificent 14th century St. Vitus Cathedral. To its south is the 13th century Lesser Quarter, where the workmen lived. On the east bank is the Old Town with its enormous, central Old Town Square. The New Town, built in the 14th century, curves around the Old Town and Wenceslas Square, the site of many political events.

Prague is one of Europe's most popular tourist destinations. With a population of around 1,220,000, it is also home to an expanding artistic community spanning the visual and literary arts and the music scene.

An aerial view of the Old Town Square in Prague.

BRNO has a population of around 400,000 and is the second largest city in the Czech Republic. Dating from the Great Moravian empire, Brno became the capital of Moravia in the 14th century. For many centuries the city remained staunchly Catholic in a mainly Protestant country, eventually becoming Protestant in the late 1500s. During the Austro-Hungarian empire, it developed a strong textile industry. In the 1920s a university was founded in the city. Today it is known for the many trade fairs held at the exhibition grounds, and the annual motorcycle grand prix.

OLOMOUC Legend has it that Julius Caesar founded Olomouc. In the 11th century, after the unification of Bohemia and Moravia, Olomouc became a major seat of administrative power. It was the capital of Moravia for several centuries in the Middles Ages. Today it is home to 100,000 Czechs. The town sits on a gentle curve of the Morava River. Olomouc, a university town, has historic architecture only second to Prague. The town has

Baroque-style fountains with classic names: Hercules, Caesar, Mercury, Neptune, and Jupiter. Cobbled streets wind through squares built in the Renaissance, Baroque, and Empire styles.

KARLOVY VARY Situated in the protected Slavkov Forest in the northwest, 1,476 feet (450 m) above sea level, Karlovy Vary is the oldest of the Bohemian spa towns. Its 12 springs are located in or near colonnaded buildings. Legend says that Charles IV was hunting in the nearby woods when his dog was scalded by a rising jet of hot water. Mineral springs are believed to possess medicinal properties, so Charles IV built a hunting lodge near the biggest spring and gave the town his name, Carlsbad. The town developed a vibrant cultural life. Goethe visited often, and so did composers like Bach, Beethoven, Brahms, Wagner, and Liszt. The annual Dvořák Music Festival attracts many visitors in September and modern art movements such as Art Nouveau have been centered here.

The spa town of Karlovy Vary was formerly called Carlsbad.

HISTORY

THE HISTORY OF THE CZECH LANDS AND PEOPLE is over 1,000 years old, and is replete with conquests and foreign rule. The Czechs have enjoyed independent statehood since January 1, 1993. The path that brought them there is a complex and fascinating one.

EARLY TRACES OF CIVILIZATION

Humans inhabited the Czech lands more than 600,000 years ago. Evidence exists of established farming communities in the lowlands from approximately 4,000 B.C. Celtic and Germanic tribes were the first people to inhabit the area.

THE GREAT MORAVIAN EMPIRE

By A.D. 600 the Slavic ancestors of today's Czechs had settled in the area, calling themselves Moravians, after the Morava River. They united under Mojmír I, who ruled from 818 to 846. His Great Moravian empire included modern-day western Slovakia, Bohemia, Silesia, parts of eastern Germany, southeastern Poland, and northern Hungary. Archeological remains have been discovered in Moravia dating to this period.

During the reign of the second ruler of the Moravian empire, Rostislav, who is also referred to as Ratislav (846–870), the written Slavic language came into existence. At Rostislav's request, the Byzantine emperor in Constantinople sent monks to introduce Christianity to the region.

The missionaries Constantine (later renamed Cyril) and Methodius arrived in 863 with a Bible written in the Cyrillic alphabet. As part of their missionary work in the region, they not only preached in Slavic but translated the Bible into the Slavic language then in use. To do this, Constantine created the Slavic alphabet. Their work was the first example of Slavic in written form.

The Romans named Bohemia after a 5th century B.C. Celtic tribe, the Boii— "Boiohemum" in Latin.

Opposite: **St. Nicholas Church in Prague's Old Town Square was completed in 1735. It was built on the site of the first church in the country, which was commissioned by German merchants in the 13th century.**

ST. WENCESLAS

Wenceslas I (c. 903?–929?), duke of Bohemia, was one of the early Přemysl rulers. Václav, as he was named, succeeded his father, chief of the Czech tribe occupying the western part of Central Bohemia, in 921, but his mother Drahomíra ruled as regent until 924 or 925. During his reign, Wenceslas extended his dominion in Bohemia. Czechs consider him the founder of the Czech state, although the Slavic tribes did not become a cohesive force until after his death. He was an educated man, and legends stress his Christian values. His submission to German King Henry I the Fowler may be the reason why his brother Boleslav conspired to murder him in 929. His murder was viewed as martyrdom, and by the beginning of the 11th century he had acquired sainthood. St. Wenceslas is today the patron saint of Bohemia.

Czech legend has it that St. Wenceslas lies sleeping, with other Czech knights, under Blanik Mountain in Bohemia. One day, it is said, they will rise under his leadership and return to free the nation of its enemies. During anti-government demonstrations in November 1989, the statue of St. Wenceslas became a shrine to the people. On the night the resignation of the Communist Party's general secretary was announced, some people chanted, "The knights of Blanik have arrived!"

Many Germans settled in Bohemia during the Přemysl dynasty.

THE PŘEMYSL DYNASTY

According to tradition, the Přemysl dynasty was founded in A.D. 800 by a plowman, Přemysl. By 950, the German king, Otto I, had conquered Bohemia and made it part of the Holy Roman empire. The Přemysl dynasty ruled Bohemia on the German kings' behalf until it fell in 1306 with the assassination of Wenceslas III. In the latter years of the dynasty the Přemysls were responsible for uniting the tribes of Bohemia and completing the region's conversion to Christianity.

The Přemysl dynasty was succeeded by the Luxembourg dynasty, whose first ruler was John of Luxembourg.

BOHEMIA'S GOLDEN AGE

Bohemia's golden age occurred under the eldest son of John of Luxembourg, Wenceslas, who changed his name to Charles and ruled from 1346 to 1378. He was crowned Emperor Charles IV in Rome in 1355. As the new seat of the Holy Roman empire, Prague became one of Europe's most important cities politically and culturally, attracting French, Italian, and German scholars, architects, scientists, and artists.

During Charles's reign, several of Prague's most significant Gothic buildings were constructed, including St. Vitus Cathedral and Charles University. Charles Bridge, which he ordered built, is still the main link today between the east and west banks of the capital.

Charles had a great gift for diplomacy, and during his reign there was harmony between the church, the throne, and the nobility. His son, Wenceslas IV, lacked this gift. During his rule, a reform movement grew, led by Jan Hus, the rector at Bethlehem Chapel. The chapel is significant for another reason—its services were conducted exclusively in Czech.

Above: **Charles IV was known as the patron of arts and sciences.**

Left: **A view of Hradčany, a castle on the west bank of Prague. Its foundations were laid in the 10th century, and it was enlarged during the reign of Charles IV. St. Vitus Cathedral is in the castle grounds.**

THE HAPSBURG DYNASTY

The Hapsburgs, a German royal family whose name derives from the Hapsburg Castle in Switzerland, provided rulers for the Holy Roman empire, Austria, and Spain. In 1526, the Catholic Hapsburg dynasty took possession of the Czech lands. Prague soon became the seat of the empire, and consequently its intellectual and artistic heart. However, the Hapsburgs failed to fulfill their promise of religious tolerance. Indignant over this, but perhaps even more over the loss of privileges, the Protestant Czech upper classes provoked what came to be known as the Thirty Years' War. The war left Bohemia's economy in ruins and brought destruction to much of central Europe. The Protestant Czechs were defeated at the Battle of the White Mountain in 1620. The battle consolidated Hapsburg rule and stripped Czechs of their independence, individual rights and property, and religious freedom. Czechs were forced to become Catholics. When the Hapsburgs moved the capital back to Vienna, Prague was reduced, culturally and economically, to a provincial town for more than a century.

THE CZECH NATIONAL REVIVAL MOVEMENT

Nationalist sentiments swept much of Europe during the late 18th and 19th centuries. With more Czechs educated due to the educational reforms instituted by the Hapsburg empress, Maria Theresa, a vocal middle class emerged. Economic reforms forced Czech laborers into bigger towns and diminished the influence of the German minorities there.

The revival movement in Prague found expression in literature, theater, and journalism. The leaders of the movement were not political figures but historians and linguists, and the key issues at first were the rights of Czechs to speak and develop a literature in their own language. Although they were defeated, the Czechs continued to push for political independence and the right to use their own language.

THE FIRST REPUBLIC

Many Czechs and Slovaks fought against the Germans and Austrians during World War I. On October 28, 1918, an independent Czechoslovak republic, called The First Republic, was declared with the support of the Allied nations. Prague was designated its capital city and Tomáš Garrigue Masaryk its first president. It was ruled by a coalition of Czech and Slovak parties, and its charter guaranteed equal rights to all citizens. Today, Czechs proudly refer to The First Republic as the only liberal democracy at the time in central Europe.

In the first two years of The First Republic, the question of the borders separating the republic from Austria, Germany, and Poland were settled.

Opposite, top: **A monument to Jan Hus stands in the middle of the Old Town Square in Prague. It was erected in 1915 to commemorate the 500th anniversary of the reformer's death.**

Opposite, bottom: **The Thirty Years' War (1618–48) began with a Bohemian custom known as defenestration. In this, Prague rebels threw the king's representatives out the window of the Bohemian chancellery in Hradčany Castle.**

Edvard Beneš (right) was foreign minister before he succeeded Tomáš Masaryk (left) when the latter retired as president in 1935. After Beneš went into voluntary exile in 1938, France and Britain at first did not recognize him. This changed in 1940, after the fall of France to the Germans. In 1943 Beneš signed a treaty of alliance with Moscow, and in March 1945, the exiles worked out a program of postwar reconstruction of their country by the Soviet Union.

THE DARK DAYS OF WORLD WAR II

By the 1930s, three million German speakers lived in Bohemia and most succumbed to Adolf Hitler's vision of a greater Germany. The British and French governments pressured Czechoslovakia into giving up Sudetenland, the northwest region of Bohemia adjoining Germany. They believed this sacrifice would appease Hitler and avoid a war. Opposing this move, President Edvard Beneš resigned on October 1, 1938 and went into exile, first in London, then in Chicago.

As history demonstrated, Hitler was not appeased. On March 14, 1939, Slovakia was also annexed. This was followed the next day by the German occupation of Bohemia and Moravia, which the Germans named the Protectorate of Bohemia and Moravia. The government of Czechoslovakia became a puppet government acting on German orders. In the period of Nazi repression that followed, Jews were targeted, but other Czechs did not escape persecution. In May 1942, after the assassination of Reinhard Heydrich, a Nazi persecutor, by unknown attackers, the Gestapo shot all the male inhabitants of the mining village of Lidice, accusing them of sheltering the assassins. The women were sent to concentration camps and the children were given to German families.

As a result of talks between the exiles, including Beneš, and the Soviet Union, the Red Army had great influence on the Czechoslovakian underground movement against the Germans. On May 5, 1945, the people rose up against the German occupiers, and by May 8, after fierce fighting, most of Prague had been liberated. US forces arrived first, but allowed the Soviet army to enter Prague as its liberator on May 9.

POST-WAR COMMUNISM

In the 1946 election, the Communist Party was the dominant party in the coalition group that formed the government, with Klement Gottwald as prime minister. Tensions soon developed between communist and non-communist cabinet members.

In February 1948, the Communist Party took over the government by force, with the military backing of the Soviet Union. A new constitution was created in May, giving the Communist Party total control. Beneš resigned rather than sanction it, and Gottwald was elected president by the national assembly in July 1948. Industry and agriculture were nationalized. Thousands of people fled the country and many leading figures in Czechoslovak society were imprisoned, executed, or died in labor camps. The 1950s was an era of harsh political repression and economic decline.

Before World War II Czechoslovakia enjoyed the 10th highest standard of living in the world. By the end of the 1980s, it had slipped to 42nd place, well below many Third World countries.

Girls from the Czech Youth Group helping to clear the rubble and re-build Prague City Hall after World War II.

PRAGUE SPRING

Civil liberties increased and censorship restrictions were loosened during the 1960s, especially toward the end of the decade under the new president, Alexander Dubček. This period of greater freedoms is known as the Prague Spring. Soviet bloc leaders became very concerned by the move toward greater democracy, and on August 20–21, 1968, Warsaw Pact troops and tanks invaded the country.

In the following decade thousands of Communist Party members were expelled from the party and lost their jobs. Typically, many educated professionals were forced to earn a living doing menial jobs. This was followed in the 1980s by economic and political stagnation, corruption of the state system, and lowered living standards—all of which contributed to a growing dissatisfaction with the communist regime.

Invasion of Prague by tanks of the Warsaw Pact troops.

THE VELVET REVOLUTION

In 1977 the country's intellectuals signed a petition known as Charter 77, listing their grievances against the repressive communist regime. It failed, but in the decade that followed, members of this group played a role in fomenting dissatisfaction against the regime. Toward the end of 1989, the citizens of Czechoslovakia began to express strong discontent with the communist regime.

The first of several demonstrations took place on August 21, 1989, the 21st anniversary of the crushing of the Prague Spring. The demonstrators—a mix of young and old, intellectuals and laborers—sang the national anthem and waved the national flag as they demanded freedom of expression, thought, association, and belief. Censorship had controlled all aspects of their lives. They wanted freedom to decide what music to play and what books to read without fear of government reprisal.

On November 17, 1989, the anniversary of the death of nine students killed by the Nazis in 1939, Prague's communist youth organized an officially sanctioned demonstration in Wenceslas Square in Prague. This square is the symbolic heart of the country, and it is where the statue of the country's patron saint stands.

For one week in November 1989, 750,000 citizens protested, demanding the resignation of the government.

The students declared an indefinite strike and were joined by actors and musicians. A week of demonstrations followed in Prague in which, in a city of two million, over 750,000 people participated. On November 27, ten days after the student strike, a general strike was held; over half the population stopped work for two hours.

President Václav Havel (left) had a theatrical career before becoming president. Here he is seen with Alexander Dubček, who made a comeback to parliament 19 years after he was removed from government for his "experiments" with democracy.

The strike precipitated the resignation of the communist chairman of the Federal Assembly and heralded the fall of the communist government. On December 28, 1989, Václav Havel was elected president and Alexander Dubček was made the speaker of parliament. The days that followed came to be called the "Velvet Revolution" because there were no casualties. The negative aspect of its "bloodless" nature is that communist leaders were not prosecuted for their crimes, while many dissidents who had fought the communist regime remained in prison.

Following the overthrow of communism, the new government had two main objectives: to ensure the first free elections since 1946 and to make a rapid push toward a free-market economy. This process involved the return of property to its original owners (pre-1948) and the privatization of most state-owned industry.

The Czechs in general were more in favor of radical economic reform than the Slovaks. This was because the Slovaks were suffering greater economic hardship and higher unemployment from a declining arms industry. Another issue was the underlying resentment the Slovaks felt at being treated as second-class citizens for many decades. These sentiments were fuelled by the election of the Movement for a Democratic Slovakia in June 1992 in Slovakia. Its leader, Vladimír Mečiar, was a strong supporter of complete independence for Slovaks and slower economic reform. The Civic Democratic Party won the election in the Czech lands. During post-election negotiations between the two parties, Václav Klaus, leader of the Civic Democratic Party, insisted on separation. In a referendum, one million Czechoslovaks supported a split.

THE VELVET DIVORCE

Václav Havel resigned in protest, refusing to preside over the split. Relations between the two republics were initially determined by 25 interstate treaties providing a framework for issues such as the division of property, federal institutions, and a common currency during the first few months after independence. Prague became the capital of the Czech Republic, Václav Havel was once again elected the president, and Václav Klaus became prime minister. Both occupy the same positions in 1998.

The positive consequences of economic reform have been booming tourism, a solid industrial base, low unemployment, shops full of products, and the restoration of city buildings. In contrast, the country is also experiencing a severe housing shortage, steeply rising crime, severe pollution, and a deteriorating health system.

By the time of partition in 1993, the Czech economy was largely market-orientated. New service-oriented industries and merchandising became increasingly important.

Jubilation over the "divorce" that created two new republics. On January 19, 1993, the Czech Republic became a member of the United Nations.

GOVERNMENT

FROM 1948 UNTIL 1989, the former Republic of Czechoslovakia was a communist state with a one-party system. Since the overthrow of the communist regime in 1989, the Czechs and Slovaks have decided to go their separate ways, after 71 years of joint statehood. The Czech Republic officially began its political, judicial, and civil life on January 1, 1993, as an independent state based on a system of parliamentary democracy.

THE LEGISLATURE

The president is the head of state, and is elected for a term of five years. However, it is the prime minister and the cabinet who wield the most power. The prime minister is chosen by the president and advises him on the selection of the other cabinet members. The cabinet consists of the prime minister, two deputy prime ministers, and ministers.

The president of the Czech Republic, Václav Havel, has occupied this position since 1993 and has presided over his country at a time of momentous change—the fall of communism, the end of a 71-year-old state and the creation of two separate republics, as well as the transformation of his country from a socialist state to a free-market, democratic state.

Václav Klaus, the prime minister, is the leader of the Civic Democratic Party, the dominant party in the coalition formed after the June 1992 elections. In the same elections, Vladimír Mečiar, the leader of the Movement for Democratic Slovakia, became the Slovakian prime minister. The Czechoslovak federation ended after these elections.

Above: **A bust of Klement Gottwald, the Czech president who eliminated opponents to the Communist Party line in the early 1950s.**

Opposite: **The First Czechoslovak Republic was proclaimed at Municipal House.**

THE PRESIDENT

The current president of the Czech Republic is Václav Havel, a former playwright and dissident. Born on October 5, 1936 into a bourgeois, educated family, he worked as a lab technician after graduating from high school. His heart was not in this work, however, and he subsequently found employment as a stage technician for theater. By 1960 he had become an assistant director and went on to produce his own plays as well. After 1968, his plays were banned from public performance in Czechoslovakia.

Havel became politically active and helped form the dissident movement Charter 77, which became a police target. Members of Charter 77 were looked upon as troublemakers by some of the populace, who were content to enjoy the availability of more goods and ignore the censorship and civil restrictions that had become a part of their life. He was imprisoned several times and continued to write from there. When not in prison, he was constantly followed by government supporters. He is renowned for his civility even toward those who sought to repress him. A story is told about one of his visits to the public baths. On his way there, he greeted the two government security men, as he always did. Just as he was about to enter the baths, the men approached him and asked if he would wait for approximately 30 minutes for two younger men to enter the baths with him, as they had heart conditions. He agreed to their request.

He took an active part in the 1989 pro-democracy demonstrations, and together with Václav Klaus, he was one of the founding members of the Civic Forum Party, which took office after the downfall of the communist government.

Havel holds deep-seated convictions regarding the inalienable rights of all people to democracy, freedom, and individual rights. After seven years, in 1998, Havel is still immensely popular. Although his popularity rating has dropped from 85% to 65%, he continues to have formidable support. His civility, honesty, and respect for civil liberties inspire a level of respect unusual in the world of Western politics. Czechs like to compare their leader to Vladimír Mečiar, the Moscow-trained leader of the Slovak Republic, who is a former boxer.

A NEW CONSTITUTION

The constitution of the Czech Republic, establishing the country as a parliamentary democracy, was adopted on December 16, 1992 by the Czech National Council. It came into effect on January 1, 1993, to coincide with the commencement of the new republic. Many of its Western liberal principles are similar to those of the constitution for the non-communist, post-1989 federation of Czechoslovakia, which was written in a very difficult period, amid tension and differences of opinion between the Czech and Slovakian leaders. The Czechs have enshrined in their constitution their respect and desire for democracy and freedom, as well as their responsibilities as individual citizens and as a community.

The process began in the June 1990 elections that decided the political leadership: the Civic Forum movement headed by Václav Havel and the Slovakian leader, Vladimír Mečiar. Apart from writing a new constitution, the new government had to make economic plans, and consider new directions in the foreign policy. When it was clear that there would be little consensus in economic reform, and separation was inevitable, Havel resigned and the Civic Forum fell apart. Meanwhile, by June 1991, the Soviet troops that were part of the Warsaw Pact had withdrawn from Czechoslovakia.

Václav Klaus was the finance minister before the 1992 election that made him the prime minister of the Czech Republic.

THE PREAMBLE OF THE CONSTITUTION

"We, the citizens of the Czech Republic in Bohemia, Moravia, and Silesia, at this time of the reconstitution of an independent Czech State, true to all the sound traditions of the ancient statehood of the Lands of the Czech Crown as well as of Czechoslovak statehood, resolve to build, protect, and advance the Czech Republic in the spirit of the inalienable values of human dignity and freedom as the home of equal and free citizens who are aware of their obligations toward others and of their responsibility to the community ..."

The oldest secular monument in Brno is the Old Town Hall.

THE HOUSES OF PARLIAMENT

The constitution allows for a parliament with two chambers—the senate (or upper house) and the chamber of deputies. Czech citizens age 18 years and older have the right to vote.

The chamber of deputies consists of 200 deputies who are elected for a term of four years. Elections are held by secret ballot and according to proportional representation. Czech citizens age 21 and older may be elected to the chamber of deputies.

The senate has 81 senators who are elected for a term of six years. One third of the senators are elected every two years. Senators are elected by secret ballot according to the principles of the majority system. Czech citizens 40 years of age and above may be elected to the senate. The Czech government functioned without an upper house from January 1993 until late 1995. The senate came into being in 1995–96, in time for the 1996 election.

WHO'S IN POWER?

The last parliamentary elections were held in 1996. Czechs expressed their dissatisfaction with government policies, and the election ended in a political deadlock: the government coalition won 52 of the 81 seats in the senate, and 99 of the 200 seats in the chamber of deputies.

The Civic Democratic Party has dominated the government coalition since July 1992. It is led by Václav Klaus, and its ideology is right-wing. This means that it supports a free-market economy and privatization with limited government interference. The other two parties that make up the coalition are the Civic Democratic Alliance and the Christian Democratic Union-Czechoslovak People's Party. Both are also right-wing groups.

The Czech Republic is divided into eight administrative centers: Prague, Bohemia (East, South, West, North, and Central Bohemia), and Moravia (North and South Moravia). These centers are further subdivided into districts, and the districts into local communities.

A CONTROVERSIAL SYMBOL

The traditional flag of the Czech lands had two equal horizontal bands of white and red. As this is identical to the flags of other former Soviet bloc countries, the Czech Republic chose to use the flag of The First Republic, which has an isosceles triangle of blue, with its base on the hoist side, wedged into the two horizontal bands. This choice created a storm of controversy with Slovakia, as the two republics had agreed not to use the old federal symbols.

A T-shirt depicts the division of Czechoslovakia.

Uniformed police in the Czech Republic.

JUDICIARY

The judicial system is determined by a law passed in July 1991, which allows for the establishment of a 15-member constitutional court and a supreme administrative court. The president appoints the judges of the supreme and constitutional courts and the senate approves his nominations.

There are civil, criminal, commercial, and administrative courts. When disputes are related to business, the people concerned go to a commercial court to settle matters. Administrative courts are courts of appeal for citizens who question the legality of decisions made in state institutions.

The courts under the Ministry of Justice have a clear hierarchy: they are at republic, region, and district levels. The first point of appeal is the district court, where cases are usually decided by a panel consisting of a judge and two associate judges. Associate judges are citizens of good standing over the age of 24, elected for four years. The regional courts deal with more serious cases, and also act as a court of appeal for district courts. In both district and regional courts, a single judge rather than a panel of judges will occasionally decide the case.

Military courts are convened under the jurisdiction of the Ministry of Defense. The supreme court interprets the law, acts as a guide to other courts, and also functions as a court of appeal.

MILITARY FORCES

Military duty is compulsory for Czech men, and service with the Reserves continues until age 60. In 1990, the length of service was reduced from two years to 18 months, and then to 12 months in 1993. Czechs have the option of performing 27 months of non-military duty instead.

The Czech Republic has a total of 90,000 personnel in the armed forces. Besides the army and air force, there are also civil defense, railroad, and internal security units. The president of the republic is the military commander-in-chief. Under the communist regime, the military was substantially larger, numbering approximately 200,000 personnel on active duty. In 1993 the new Czech Republic government had the intention of reducing the size of the armed forces to 65,000 personnel by December 1995. Those plans were suspended indefinitely in response to the Russian Federation's decision to abandon its own plans for reductions. Since 1994, the republic has increased its annual expenditure for defense, from the equivalent of US$746 million in 1993 to US$823 million in 1995.

Dividing the troops in the former Federal Army, as part of the partition process, was a formidable task. Stationing troops along the Czech-Slovak border is prohibited.

Guards on duty outside the Hradčany Castle in Prague.

ECONOMY

THE CZECH REPUBLIC'S economy has experienced many fundamental changes since the communist regime ended in 1989. In 1990, the finance minister of Czechoslovakia, Václav Klaus (now the prime minister of the Czech Republic), instigated a wide-ranging series of reforms designed to bring about a free-market economy. The results so far have been varied.

The Czech Republic's industrial base includes the production of steel, iron, cement, ceramics, plastics, cotton, clothing, and beer. The timber industry provides most of the timber required for newsprint, furniture, plywood, and traditional woodworking. The government continues to own 45% or 6,422,000 acres (2.6 million hectares) of all forests, while the remaining 55% have been returned to their pre-1948 owners.

TWO PHASES OF REFORM

Klaus instigated a privatization plan that consisted of two phases. The first phase required the return of property to pre-1948 owners or their descendants and the sale of enterprises through auctions or direct to foreign buyers. This phase has been quite successful, with almost 16,500 units privatized and 183 units returned to former owners. Over 80% of enterprises has been privatized. As a result, most restaurants, hotels, and retail stores are now privately owned, while the government still owns most theaters, museums, and castles. Banks continue to be state-run, and it may be some time before they, too, are privatized.

The second phase concentrated on large-scale industries and small enterprises that had not found buyers. A coupon system was introduced to give every citizen the chance to become a shareholder. After January 1994, the coupons could be exchanged for shares in over 770 companies. The idea was greeted enthusiastically by most Czechs and Slovaks at the time, with 8.5 million people buying coupons.

On January 1, 1993, when the Czech Republic officially became an independent state, it also became a member of the International Monetary Fund, the World Bank, the European Bank for Reconstruction and Development, and the Conference on Security and Cooperation in Europe (CSCE). The path to capitalism had begun in earnest.

Opposite: **Temelín nuclear cooling station. Nuclear power plants here and in Dukovany provide an alternative source of energy production and reduced the country's reliance on coal-mining.**

THE PRIME MINISTER

Václav Klaus is the key figure in the Czech Republic's move from a socialist ideology to a Western-style democratic, market-driven economy. A founding member of the Civic Forum, the party that took office after the fall of the communist regime in 1989, Klaus served as the finance minister of Czechoslovakia. He has been the prime minister of the Czech Republic since 1992.

Born in 1941 in Prague, he studied international economic relations and international trade at the Prague School of Economics, from which he graduated in 1963. He did his postgraduate studies in Italy and at Cornell University in the United States. Until 1970, when he was forced to leave for political reasons, he worked as a researcher at the Institute of Economics of the Czechoslovak Academy of Sciences. In 1987, he was allowed to return to the Academy of Sciences.

His party's popularity has declined as economic hardships have continued, and his detractors describe him as aggressive and arrogant. The speed of privatization has also raised uncomfortable questions for his government. Lawyers did not play a key role in formulating the relevant laws; consequently, legal loopholes have allowed high level corruption and quick profits by the unscrupulous. This has caused public ill-will toward the government.

Of the total labor force, 44% is in services, 33% in industry, 9% in construction, 7% in agriculture, and 7% in transportation and communications.

Today, the second phase is focusing on the return of property to the Catholic Church, the implementation of a bankruptcy law, and the privatization of agriculture and health care.

AGRICULTURE IN DECLINE

Agriculture is one of the biggest problems facing the government today. Crop production has declined since the late 1980s. Under communism, land that had been private property became state property, and it was then extensively cultivated. Farmers did not have to work hard, as communism guaranteed them a wage, regardless of how much they produced. Since the farm was state-owned, they did not have to make it commercially viable. Consequently, if farm machinery broke down, this was seen as fortunate, as the farmer could not work until the equipment was repaired. Repairs often took weeks.

Today, many Czechs cannot claim their land because it is impossible to determine which section of it was once theirs. Many are reluctant to make a claim, anyway, because to make the land financially viable will

require much effort and investment. Ironically, many owners of small plots are joining cooperatives in order to make a living. It will be many years before the land becomes productive once again, and there is still a shortage of appropriate technology on the smaller farms.

Although the country has ample fertile land and resources, it is not self-sufficient in food. A basic problem is organization and distribution. Fruit on the trees in the countryside remains unpicked while grapes imported from Spain are sold in the city streets. It may be simply a question of time before agriculture absorbs the effects of the rapid economic changes and reduced labor force and becomes a successful sector once again.

The major crops are sugar beets, wheat, potatoes, corn, barley, rye, and hops. The preferred livestock are cattle, pigs, chickens, and horses. The dairy industry continues to supply most domestic requirements. South Bohemia has a well-established fish farm industry, consisting mainly of carp. These carp lakes were excavated during the Middle Ages and carp is a traditional dish at Christmas.

A field of rapeseed, an important cash crop for the country.

RESOURCES AND ENERGY

There are limited reserves of coal, coke, timber, lignite, uranium, and iron ore in the Czech Republic. Central Bohemia, between Prague and Plzeň, is an important region for iron-ore mining. Lead and zinc ore are mined near Kutná Hora and Příbram in Bohemia and in the northeast of the country; uranium in Příbram and in the northern regions of Bohemia; and tin in the Ore Mountains to the northeast.

The major centers for coal-mining and manufacturing have traditionally been in the northern regions of Bohemia. Severe air pollution, a side-effect of burning low-quality brown coal, is a serious problem there. At present, most electricity comes from coal-burning plants and the

In the south, the discovery of copper, gold, and silver deposits attracted the growth of mining communities.

AN ECONOMIC REPORT CARD

In April 1993 the Prague Stock Exchange was reopened amid optimism for the new market economy. But it has been a rocky economic path since the Velvet Divorce. Exports to Slovakia dropped by 50% in the first three months of 1993. Inflation was at 59%. By 1996, it had been reduced to 8.7%, which was still higher than the European Union (EU) average. Unemployment has remained stable: it was 3.2% in 1993 and 3.3% three years later.

Since 1989, however, the government has succeeded in delivering a balanced budget every year. Foreign investment in Czech companies and industry has been encouraged. Tourism is also a booming industry. Entry into the EU along with Poland, Hungary, Slovenia, and Estonia will happen before the end of the century. "Back to Europe" was one of the key slogans after the 1989 revolution. Full membership in the EU has been the goal of the present government from the time it entered office.

ENVIRONMENTAL POLLUTION

Parts of the republic are among the most polluted in the world. The concentration of light industry in northern Bohemia and Moravia since the industrial revolution has been exacerbated by the introduction of heavy industry during the communist years. The burning of low-grade brown coal is primarily responsible for the 1,542,800 tons (1,400,000 metric tonnes) of sulfur that industry emits annually. Acid rain has affected 60% of all the forests in the country.

Prague is the site of some of the worst air pollution in the country. In the winter, when people are using their home furnaces and power plants are running at peak production, the pollution can reach dangerous levels. Residents are sometimes advised not to leave their homes.

According to World Bank statistics, 3% of deaths in the Czech Republic are due to air pollution, while child deaths due to respiratory diseases are 2.4 times higher in polluted areas than unpolluted ones. Many people feel that the government is not doing all it can. Public attention tends to be more focused on creating a better standard of living than on the environment.

In the Czech Republic, North Bohemia is most at risk from air pollution, followed by North Moravia and the region of Prague. In North Bohemia, children are given gas masks and life expectancy is five years less than elsewhere in the country.

nuclear reactor at Dukovany. Oil and natural gas are imported from Russia. To reduce dependency on Russia, an oil pipeline through Germany is under construction, and a nuclear power plant is scheduled to open in 1999 at Temelín. This was a communist project that the post-1989 government decided to complete, modifying the original Soviet design with Western safety technology and procedures.

This controversial project has been the subject of protests by anti-nuclear activists, including overseas environmentalists. Each year since 1993, a non-violent protest has been staged.

TRANSPORTATION

TRAINS AND BUSES After the Velvet Divorce, the old Czechoslovak state rail company was divided into the Czech Railways and the Railways of the Slovak Republic. Their combined network is among Europe's densest. Most major cities are linked by several trains a day, and travel is cheap by Western standards. Unfortunately, Czech Railways is in financial straits. For the average Czech traveler, this makes train travel more expensive than other modes of transportation and not as pleasant in terms of the cleanliness and general condition of the carriages. Privatization and integration into the European rail network should eventually improve the quality and efficiency of the railways.

Buses tend to be cheaper, faster, and more reliable than trains. Buses connect the suburbs to city centers; some cover even longer distances. Commuters purchase train and bus tickets at tobacco stands, newsstands, and ticket-vending machines in the larger cities. Timetables for public transportation can also be purchased at bookshops.

ON THE ROAD The republic has a network of good roads. Some follow old routes through villages and small towns, and may include sudden sharp bends. There are 310 miles (500 km) of West European-style highways, for which drivers purchase a motorway sticker. There are as yet no toll roads.

Only 47% of Czechs own cars, which means that highways and country roads tend to have light traffic. On the whole, Czech drivers are considerate. As in the rest of Europe, one drives on the right side of the road. The legal driving age is 18. Fines for speeding and drunk driving are very high. Car theft and the theft of valuables from cars has become a major problem in the larger cities.

IN THE AIR The Czech Republic has two airports. Ruzyně in Prague is the international airport and Ostrava in North Moravia services flights between the Czech and Slovak republics.

Generally, rivers flow too quickly to be used for passenger transportation. The one exception is the Vltava River, which sees some river traffic in the summer.

FLOODS

The floods that affected over one-third of the Czech Republic in mid-1997 not only took lives and destroyed homes but caused industries, foundries, mines, and utilities to suffer great losses from flood damage and interrupted production. The floods affected mostly northern and eastern Moravia, especially the industrial core around Ostrava. Telephone lines and power lines came down, and thousands of miles of roads were destroyed.

The floods also brought down the value of the Czech currency on the stock market. Financially, it will take some time for the republic to recover. Estimates of the total cost of damage range from 45 to 90 billion Koruna (US$1.4–2.8 billion). In order to cover the cost of damages, the government has chosen not to increase taxes, but instead has created "flood bonds" for public purchase. This income will help pay for ongoing costs.

CZECHS

THE PRESENT-DAY CZECHS are the descendants of Slavonic tribes that migrated into central Europe during the 5th and 6th centuries A.D. Those tribes inhabited the regions of Bohemia and Moravia as well as western Slovakia, eastern Germany, southern Poland (including Silesia), and northern Hungary. Several minorities make up the rest of the population. Tensions sometimes surface between the Czechs and minority groups over long-standing resentments and issues of racism.

THE ETHNIC MAKE-UP

In a population of approximately 10,300,000, 94% are ethnic Czechs and 3% are Slovaks. There are also small groups of Poles, Germans, Romanies or Gypsies, and Hungarians. The Jews form a very small but significant minority.

Opposite and left: **A woman from the town of Strážnice in Moravia and an old man from the Krkonoše (Giant) Mountains in the north.**

49

The Czechs see themselves as cultured and educated compared to the Slovaks.

THE CZECH SELF-IMAGE

Czechs and Slovaks have shared a common national history that began after World War I and ceased with the creation of two separate republics in 1993. (There was also a period in the 9th century, when they came together in a state called Great Moravian empire, but that was too long ago to have left a lasting impact.) During their recent joint history, Slovaks have perceived themselves as being treated by the Czechs as second-class citizens. There is a commonly held notion among Czechs that Slovaks are the "younger brother." The Czechs continue to play the role of patron with a moral duty to guide the younger, naive brother who would otherwise lose his way. It is an attitude that has long inspired resentment.

Many Czechs appear to differentiate themselves from the Slovaks. Knowing little about the history and culture of Slovakia, they can be quick to generalize about Slovaks. Hence they describe Slovaks as uncultured, underdeveloped, socialist-tending, unsophisticated, and having a traditional (or backward) community. In contrast, many Czechs see themselves as a cultured, educated, and peace-loving people. In their minds they belong to the sophisticated, developed, and democratic West. They see their socialist history as an aberration, an alien influence from the East more appropriate for the Slovaks than for themselves. They pride themselves on their democratic traditions, their love of freedom and individual rights, and on the enthusiasm with which they have pursued capitalism and free-market goals since the Velvet Revolution.

The Czech Self-image

Czechs are also extremely sensitive about being categorized as Eastern Europeans, for they associate Eastern Europeans as backward, both socially and culturally. They are quick to point out the geographically central location of the republic and the fact that Prague is more west than Vienna. This is perhaps one of the reasons they were keen to identify with Western Europe.

They have a contradictory mix of high-minded ideals and very human frailties. A 1992 sociological survey of stereotypes of the Czech character found that 76% of the self-traits most often mentioned by Czechs interviewed were negative: enviousness, excessive conformity, cunning, egoism, laziness, cowardice, quarrelsomeness, hypocrisy, haughtiness, and devotion to pleasure and sensuous enjoyment. Positive characteristics listed were: hardworking, skillful, and having a sense of humor. Yet when Czechs speak of themselves as a nation, they speak of a democratic, cultured, well-educated, peace-loving nation. Everyday experiences do not necessarily color the mythical qualities of their national character.

And what is the national character of the Czech? Czechs refer to a mythologized character they call the "little Czech." This high achiever is naturally very productive, but on a small scale, like a bee. His "golden hands" cope with everything they touch; he is skillful, talented, and ingenious. He is the embodiment of ordinariness and common sense. He is also an ambivalent character, because despite his ingenuity and initiative, he shuns high ideals and chooses to pour all his energies into his family and home. These qualities, some say, are what helped Czechs survive times of oppression and foreign rule. Others see this mythical figure as the embodiment of all that is negative in many Czechs—Czechs, they say, are quick to point out negative traits in others, yet slow to recognize the same in themselves.

A paradox exists among the Czechs: despite their tendency to look down upon the Slovaks, a strong egalitarian ethos pervades Czech culture. Czechs emphasize the fact that everyone is good at something, which shows sympathy for the idea of equality for all human beings.

Carrying the shopping home in Strážnice, Moravia. It is mostly the older Czechs who wear traditional clothes.

MINORITIES

GERMANS This is one of the large minority groups in the Czech Republic, with a population of approximately 50,000. During World War II, however, there were 3.2 million Germans in the Czech lands and Slovakia.

Germanic tribes arrived in the region before the Slavs, establishing farming communities around 4,000 B.C. Since then, Germans have been a continuous presence in Czech history, often taking the role of the traditional enemy. Although the Austro-Hungarian empire was good economically for the Czech lands, culturally it was stifling. The rulers progressively forced German language and culture on the population until Prague and the other large Czech cities were essentially German cities. In contrast, the German minority was treated well during The First Republic, between 1918 and 1938. The First Republic was a rich country during those years of peace. The Germans had their own schools and even their own university in Prague.

Nazi Germany irrevocably destroyed the social fabric in Czechoslovakia when it took possession of Sudetenland, then later occupied the regions of Bohemia and Moravia. The Nazi reign of terror brought retaliation against all Germans after World War II, when the Czechs expelled the German minority from Czechoslovakia. Three million Germans were forced out of the country, literally overnight, leaving behind property and lucrative businesses, especially in the industrial heartland of Bohemia. These were expropriated by the government. Some 200,000 Germans died in the hardship of the march out

of the country, from massacres, exhaustion, and suicide. Resentment and grievances continue to color the relations between the two countries. In January 1996, the Czech foreign minister and his German counterpart met in Bonn to improve relations, but failed to resolve long-standing issues.

GYPSIES The Gypsies form a group of approximately 31,000 in the Czech Republic. Before the split into two republics, there were one million Gypsies in all of Czechoslovakia. Gypsies are thought to be descendants of migrants from India in the 15th century. They have been marginalized throughout Europe; such is the case in the Czech Republic.

The Gypsy population sharply increased since the 1950s, due to births and those migrating into Czechoslovakia in search of work, many filling vacancies left by Germans who had been forced to leave. The communist government attempted to integrate them into the local society, with limited success. Czechs today are dismissive of the Gypsies. The mayor of one of Prague's districts was quoted in a newspaper as supporting the idea of moving them out of Prague's central districts to the outskirts.

Gypsies or Romanies dressed for a festival. Since the 1989 revolution, life has become intolerable for the Gypsies in the Czech Republic and Slovakia.

The Jewish quarter in Prague is known as the Josefov. The first Jewish settlement in Prague was founded in 1091.

VIETNAMESE The minorities include, interestingly, a small community of Vietnamese who run market stalls and other small businesses. They were brought over during the communist era as guest workers on aid programs. When the aid programs ended, they refused to return to Vietnam and have since faced racism, poor working conditions, and pressure from a government that wants to repatriate them. Czechs grudgingly admire their business acumen and work ethos.

THE JEWS

Jews have had a constant presence in Czech culture since establishing themselves in Prague in the 11th century. The persecution of Jews during World War II saw the emigration of 19,000 Jews, and the murder of nearly 80,000. Only 6,000 Jews remain in the Czech Republic, mainly in the Josefov quarter of Prague. Anti-Semitism continues in the Czech Republic, and police have been accused of inaction. Public protest has seen some police officers expelled from the force.

In 1997, Czech leaders finally agreed to compensate Slovak Jews for gold and other valuables that the fascist regime had confiscated from Slovak Holocaust victims in World War II. The valuables had been deposited in the Czechoslovak State Bank in 1953 and assimilated into the federal budget. Approximately 19 million Koruna (US$590,000) will be paid into a foundation run by Jewish organizations. The Czech government will pay two-thirds of the total, and the Slovak government the rest.

A NATION GROWING OLDER

Czechs have become primarily an urban people, with over 70% of the population living in the larger towns and cities. Urban congestion has led to smaller living spaces and an increase in living expenses, particularly rent. Traditionally, elderly parents live with their adult children when they cannot live alone for health or other reasons; this puts further pressure on available space. Contraception and abortion are widely practiced, and it is not surprising, therefore, that the rate of population growth is a negative figure: −0.13%, according to a 1997 estimate. The population is slowly aging. Perhaps due to other more urgent issues, this is not being addressed as the potential problem it is.

In 1997, 13% of the population were 65 years old and above, but the trend towards smaller families will increase this figure in the near future.

TRADITIONAL CLOTHING

Folk dress grew in popularity from the 1950s due to the efforts of the communist government to revive patriotism through folklore and folk traditions—what they called "the people's culture." Folk songs replaced the jazz of the day, young people were taught folk dances and discouraged from modern dance forms, and May Day processions were replete with traditional dress, flags, and brass bands.

Traditional folk dress is not commonly worn every day in most parts of the republic, but older people in some villages still wear them, and they always appear at folk festivals. Departing from the simple clothing, usually in drab colors, worn in everyday life, folk dress is embellished with bright and detailed embroidery work in abstract or pictorial designs.

The designs and patterns vary depending on the season, age, and marital status of the wearer. More elaborate dress evolved for church, weddings, and other special events. The dress also reflects the region—for example, in the eastern regions of the Czech Republic one sees detailed hand-sewn skirts, aprons, and shawls for both men and women, while in the west one typically sees striking shawls, belts, headgear, and shoes.

These traditional clothes are a disappearing folk tradition, which survives only through the efforts of minority cultural groups and semi-professional groups whose purpose is to promote folk culture. Most young people do not willingly participate in the folk customs that call for such clothing; it certainly lacks relevance to modern, urban living styles. Making these clothes also calls for great expense and effort, key reasons for not continuing the tradition.

A region near the German border in the northwest is still noted for wearing traditional dress. The inhabitants, called Chods, settled here about a thousand years ago. They are famous for their handicraft, which includes woodcarving and pottery. The residents make an annual pilgrimage to a mountain on the weekend following August 10, where they participate in a festival of bagpipe music and traditional song and dance.

Above: **A craftsman from the Chodsko region making bagpipes. The word "Chods" comes from the Slavic word meaning "patrols."**

Opposite: **Children in traditional Moravian dress.**

LIFESTYLE

SINCE THE OVERTHROW of communism in 1989, many influences from the socialist era can still be felt in Czech work and social life. People have been reluctant to forego some of the privileges that communism once afforded them, such as a more relaxed work routine. A measure of realism has also seeped into the Czech way of life, and people no longer expect capitalism to provide them with instant wealth.

TRANSITION TO DEMOCRACY AND CAPITALISM

In the last decade, Czechs have seen the demise of communism and a rapid move into a democratic, capitalist society along with separation from Slovakia. These events have brought many changes that have altered people's lives. But there was disappointment that instant wealth for all did not follow the introduction of capitalism, and pessimism over the rising cost of living and insufficient income.

Opposite: **Charles Bridge in Prague is a popular stopping place, whether to meet a friend or to sketch the city.**

Left: **Shopping at one of Prague's many street markets.**

The Czech's lifestyle has generally improved since 1989, with unemployment remaining low and the economy stable. New opportunities have been created in the workplace with the post-1989 policy of privatization and the establishment of new companies. However, deep-set attitudes are taking time to change. The most progressive thinking is found in entirely new private companies. In older companies that have been privatized only recently, habits from the communist regime still exist, for example, treating Friday as the beginning of the weekend.

Poor service is another throwback from the old days—in shops, some sales assistants still prefer to chat with each other rather than serve a customer, while some public servants continue to fulfill their professional duties as if it were a heavy burden. Czechs comment on the courtesy and good service they receive abroad and note their continuing absence from Czech institutions. Other negative legacies of the transition have been high-level fraud and corruption aided by inadequate legislation. Crime, especially theft, in the larger cities has risen.

Life under communism was stifling so people sought out meaning and satisfaction in their lives outside of work. Family life and friendships assumed greater importance, and pastimes such as stamp-collecting or writing poetry were

popular. The years under a communist regime created a mentality that is still very evident: people expect to get something for nothing. They still focus their energies outside of work, even though the workplace and what it represents has changed.

OPINIONS A poll taken in July 1997 of one thousand people, age 15 and above, indicated that 25% believed the situation under the former regime had been better than the present. This included many young people who had not experienced life under communism, and had probably heard their parents say that under communism rents were cheaper, that although salaries were lower, you could steal from the government, that there were fewer murders, more bread and beer for the money, and more ways to sneak around the system. Some young people recognized that the essential difference was a lack of freedom under the communists.

This poll is held regularly: in 1991, 14% of the people who were questioned held this view; in 1996, it was 18%.

Above: Street entertainers earn their meal ticket in a group performance.

Opposite: The majority of Prague's young people reject tradition, and see themselves as Westernized, liberal, and unconventional.

Apartment blocks are
popular in the cities. Private home ownership is
important to Czechs, and
an increasing shortage
of housing is a growing
problem in the cities.

HOW PEOPLE LIVE

Over 70% of Czechs live in the larger towns and cities, most of them in
apartments rather than houses. They tend to be very house-proud. Outside
the apartment door or immediately inside will be lots of shoes, or a
cupboard for shoes. Czechs usually remove their shoes at the door and put
on house slippers. Their homes often have indoor plants. These are
important as there is little space in an urban setting to enjoy a garden.
Outdoor gardening is usually done at second homes in the countryside.

People continue to struggle with the hardships of economic reality.
In 1997, rent, taxes, and the cost of public utilities, transportation, postage,
insurance, and even food rose sharply and is still increasing. Unfortunately,
this has occurred at the same time that government and some private
salaries have been capped.

In striking contrast are the nouveaux riches, often the adult children of former communist leaders, who drive around in expensive new cars and are generally ostentatious about their newfound wealth. Their family connections have enabled them to capitalize financially on the changes the country has undergone.

CITY LIVING For most Czechs, Prague is the ultimate in city living. Their appetite for going out and socializing is satisfied by the vast number of cafés, pubs, and restaurants to be visited. However, it is not just about going out for a bite. Prague buildings display an amazing array of architectural styles and decor, which makes dining out a special occasion. The Grand Hotel Europa is one example. Built in 1904, the café at ground level is crowned by an oval gallery, and polished timbers gleam throughout. Here people can sit and warm their hands on a delicious cup of hot chocolate and watch others go about their business on the busy main street outside.

Prague is one of the few cities in Europe that were not bombed during World War II, and consequently it has many beautiful old buildings. There are houses in Prague dating back at least to the early 18th century. Above their main door are signs or ornamental frames made of metal, stone, or wood. These cartouches, as they are commonly called, indicated the occupant's social rank or profession, and helped identify the building. Street numbers were introduced in 1770. Today many Czechs continue to live in such houses, sometimes inhabiting an ancestral home that has belonged to the family for centuries. Descendants of the world-renowned Art Nouveau artist Alfons Mucha continue to live in the house he inhabited when he returned from Paris in 1910. Above the first floor windows and directly above the main entrance is a large cartouche elaborately outlined in curls and contours.

Czechs take pride in their homes, and gifts such as flowers or a house plant are often proffered when visiting.

RURAL LIVING   In old farmhouses, whether they are one-bedroom shacks or two-story buildings, activities are focused around the stove. Often there is a built-in bench next to the stove for the little tasks that can be done while keeping warm, and typically the area around the stove is covered in strikingly colored ceramic tiles. Near the stove and along the wall hang enamel pots. If the house has a second story, the main bedroom is located directly above the stove in order to take advantage of its warmth.

Many country dwellings are constructed of wood. The surface of a wall is often decorated with strips of wood arranged in patterns, providing texture and interest. Window frames have elaborate designs. The preference for ornamentation is also seen in wardrobes, chests of drawers, and other furniture, which are typically painted with elaborate patterns, both abstract and figurative. Hand-embroidered bedcovers contrast beautifully with the dark tones of the wooden head and footboards. Czechs enjoy the simple pleasures of their country home, especially as a weekend or vacation retreat. They also appreciate the stillness and beauty of the countryside.

THE FAMILY

The nuclear family of parents and their children is the basic Czech family unit, and the bond between extended family members is generally lifelong. People tend not to move often, so contact between siblings after marriage remains constant.

In many families, *babička* ("BAB-ish-ka"), or the grandmother, is the key figure. Grandmothers enjoy much respect as a source of wisdom and are figures of authority. They often act as baby-sitters, as it is common for both parents to work. The legendary status of the grandmother is described in the 1855 novel *Babička* by Božena Nemcová, which is a perennial favorite with Czechs of all ages.

The Czech family is a close-knit unit.

THE ROLE OF WOMEN

Most Czech women prefer not to call themselves feminists. Those who do are usually middle-class, educated women who declare marriage changed them. Brought up to believe that they should care for the home, exposure to feminist ideas helped them realize that it was not abnormal to dislike housework.

Eighty-eight percent of Czech women of productive age work full-time and women constitute 45% of the total labor force, with 12.5% of women considering themselves sole and 48% partial breadwinners for their families. The discussion of women's rights only really surfaced in Czech society after 1989. The first public debate on feminism was broadcast on television in 1992, and a book hailed as the first Czech feminist writing appeared only in that year.

Part of the reason that feminism has not been evident in the Czech Republic may be the legacy of socialist policies. In the communist regime, women's entitlements included equal pay for work, equal educational opportunities, and six months' maternity leave at full pay. Nurseries and kindergartens were provided in local communities and in the workplace. Public institutions employed a greater number of women than in the West because of quotas set by the government.

Detractors of communist ideology argue that socialism really exploited women. By placing women in the workforce it became impossible for a family to survive on one income alone. Yet women were expected to continue to shoulder the traditional responsibilities of home and children. Despite the law on equal pay, 45% of women surveyed in 1991 reported their pay to be less than that of men for the same kind of work, and women were more likely to be fired.

Czechs do not appear to question certain premises, which greatly influences and restricts a trend toward gender equality. They see gender differences as embedded in nature and as resulting directly from the biological differences between men and women. Women emphasize their unique experience of child bearing, and both men and women argue that women's desires are almost entirely focused on the bearing and raising of children. Biological differences determine the differences in psychological dispositions. The general belief is that the typical characteristics of men naturally predispose them to be assertive, reasonable and rational, innovative, firm in their opinions, egoistic, and authoritarian. In contrast, women are perceived to be shy, tender and submissive, more emotional, less sure of their opinions, unselfish, and loving and caring. Not only Czech men but most Czech women, including some of the well-educated, seem to see the Western tendency to redefine gender roles as inappropriate for their culture. They also see it as unrealistic, because it interferes with what they believe is determined by nature. There are hardly any protests over advertisements using women to help sell a product, or with women in inferior roles, such as the housewife being told by a male scientist which washing powder is best.

Czech women are given equal opportunities for educational advancement, but their position in the workplace and in society depends on the people's perception of different priorities in male and female roles.

Above: **In a traditional wedding, the bridegroom saws wood.**

Opposite: **The Carolinum was originally a palace purchased by King Wenceslas IV for Charles University. This university, which was founded in 1348, has been added to over the centuries.**

Czech women today are primarily concerned with greater representation in politics, so that they themselves can address issues such as education, child benefits, child care, maternity benefits, and other family policy and family law issues. Many women also believe that the presence of women in parliament would make for more compassionate and honest government.

WEDDINGS

Czechs tend to marry young, especially in rural areas. A girl unmarried at 22 may be thought of as "on the shelf." Traditionally, girls were pressured to "catch" a man before he went off to complete his military service. Such pressures are declining. Folk customs are still part of village weddings. Elaborately embroidered clothes are worn, special songs and dances enjoyed, and old rituals such as the mock abduction of the bride are also carried out.

A LITERATE PEOPLE

Education in primary and secondary school, from age 6 to 16, is compulsory, and continues to be fully funded by the state today. There are also state kindergartens for children age 3–6 and secondary schools preparing students age 15–18 for university. The literacy rate is around 99%, with 41% of Czechs having finished secondary education, and 5% a college education. Czechs consider themselves to be educated people. They revere education and encourage their children to do well academically. The republic has four universities: Charles University and the Czech Technical University in Prague, Masaryk University in Brno, and Palachy University in Olomouc.

In the 1980s, expenditure on education put Czechoslovakia into 72nd place worldwide, with Nepal in the 71st. A student slogan during the Velvet Revolution was "One step further in the New Year, we shall leave Nepal behind." Information and resources available to Czechs are on par with the West, but this is offset by the students' inability to think independently, one of the legacies of the communist era. There is also a need to create new textbooks to replace the propaganda-laden communist texts that are being used even today.

When Czechs die, they are often accompanied to their final resting place by amateur woodwind bands, usually made up of members of the local fire brigade.

THE HEALTH CRISIS

The health service is undergoing drastic changes. Czechs pay 7.5% of their wages to health insurance companies for medical care. When they need medical attention, they do not pay to see a doctor. Some doctors, though, have started billing their patients for their services, claiming that the insurance companies are not paying them adequately for medical procedures. The dispute has affected all Czechs, and many have grumbled about the better days under communism when the health service was free.

Foreigners are treated by any hospital or clinic and have to pay for their own treatment. Payment for the treatment must be in foreign currency, but the medication prescribed must be paid for in Czech Korunas.

WORKING LIFE

The work day usually begins at 8 a.m. and ends anywhere between 3 and 4.30 p.m. Shops tend to be open from 8 or 9 a.m. to 5 or 6 p.m. The presence of foreign companies is extending the work day for Czechs, and

STATISTICS

(1997 estimates)

Population: 10,298,324 (male 5,008,823; female 5,289,501)

Population growth rate: −0.13%

Birth rate: 8.84 births/1,000 population

Death rate: 11.02 deaths/1,000 population

Infant mortality rate: 6.9 deaths/1,000 live births

Fertility rate: 1.17 children born/woman

they do not like it. The work week is Monday to Friday, but it is hard to achieve anything on a Friday afternoon, as many people continue to treat it as the beginning of the weekend. Most banks are open from 8 a.m. until noon, Monday through Friday, and some larger bank branches sometimes stay open until 5 p.m. On Saturdays the shops are open until noon or 1 p.m. Large department stores are an exception: they often remain open until 6 p.m.

Czechs can still be found pouring their energy and resources into their family home or country cottages, while sometimes being less than industrious at work.

A wine distiller testing wine in the wine district of Mikulov in South Moravia.

RELIGION

SINCE THE INTRODUCTION of Christianity to the Czech lands in the 9th century, Czechs have swung from Catholicism to Protestantism, and then back to Catholicism. Under the communist regime (1948–89), people were banned from expressing their religious beliefs. Their history has strongly determined the strength of Czechs' religious beliefs today, and the role religion plays in their lives.

THE CHRISTIAN EMISSARIES

The Greek monks, Cyril and Methodius, brought Christianity to the Czech lands in A.D. 863. Their work in central and eastern Europe involved translating the Bible into the local spoken language. Cyril, the younger of the two, was educated at a school for children of the Byzantine imperial family. He had a gift for languages and held prestigious positions as

Opposite: The magnificent interior of St. Vitus Cathedral in Prague.

Left: Congregation at Klokoty Monastery in Tábor, Czech Republic. Tábor was named after Mount Tábor in present-day Israel, which Christians believe to be the site of Christ's transfiguration.

73

Followers of the Hare Krishna movement assume Hindu customs and dress.

Utraquists take their name from their doctrine of the double communion—they receive both bread and wine. The Latin utraque means "each of two."

professor of philosophy at the Magnaura Palace School and as librarian of St. Sofia in Constantinople (modern Istanbul). The Greek missionary brothers belonged to the Orthodox Christian Church of Constantinople. They translated the Bible into the Slavic language of the time, causing much controversy because it was seen as heretical not to teach Christianity in one of the then holy languages—Greek, Latin, and Hebrew.

As part of the Holy Roman empire, Czechs remained loyal to the Catholic faith until the reformer and philosopher Jan Hus agitated against what he saw as corruption in the church and a need to return to early Christian principles. He was burned as a heretic in 1415, and his followers, a politico-religious group called the Hussites, started the Hussite Wars that raged from 1419 to 1434. The Hussites were divided into two groups: the Taborites and the Utraquists. The Taborites merged with another group called the Bohemian Brethren in 1457; some Utraquists merged with the Lutherans and others with the Roman Catholics. Czechs remained strongly Protestant for two more centuries, although they were part of the Holy Roman empire.

In the 17th century the Hapsburg empire rose to prominence in the Czech lands, bringing with it religious intolerance. Catholicism was forced upon the Protestant Czechs, particularly after their defeat in the Battle of the White Mountain in 1620. The religious freedom that became the norm in 1918, when Czechoslovakia came into being, lasted a relatively brief period. A communist government came into power in 1948 and declared the state officially atheist, closing most churches and imprisoning many members of the clergy. In response, some Czechs started an underground religious network that carried out services in secret and had links to the political underground movement called the Charter 77.

Czechs regained their religious freedom with the introduction of a tolerant and democratic constitution in 1990. Almost every Christian group is represented in the republic, as are other religions including Judaism, Islam, and the Hare Krishnas, a denomination of the Hindu faith.

The Pope's visit to the Czech Republic attracted large audiences of the Catholic faithful.

A SLAVIC POPE

Although historically Czechs were fiercely Protestant, Catholicism today has the firmer hold. Of the population, 39.2% are Roman Catholic while 4.6% are Protestant; the rest are Orthodox Christians (3%), other religious groups (13.4%), and atheists (39.8%).

The selection of a Pole, Pope John Paul II, as the Roman Catholic Pope, was significant for the Czechs, who felt a strong affinity with his Slavic roots, and naturally more people were drawn to the Roman Catholic Church. The Pope visited Prague in 1990, and returned to the Czech Republic again in early 1997.

Tyn Church in Prague's Old Town Square, just behind the Jan Hus monument, was the Hussites' place of worship before they were defeated by the Catholics in 1620. The present-day Czech and Slovakian Hussite Church was formed in 1920.

FADING CHRISTIANITY

Czechs do not attend church services regularly. It is mainly the elderly who go to church these days, although more children are attending religious education classes. People do not tend to discuss religious matters, as they are considered irrelevant to daily life. Despite the reduced congregation, the churches in the larger cities are crowded with the large number of tourists in them.

There appears to be a reluctance among Czechs to be devout Christians. Some Czechs have warned of the danger of the Catholic Church becoming authoritarian and hence undemocratic. This is perhaps a reaction from years of repression under communist rule; on the other hand, it could be a continuance of the atheism that was fundamental to the doctrine of communism.

The Catholic Church has been compensated by the government for church property the communist government confiscated 40 years ago. Part of those funds have gone toward restoring and maintaining Catholic churches throughout the country. There are now many beautiful churches in the countryside as well as in the cities.

The Protestants are represented by several groups in the Czech Republic, the largest being the Hussite Church, which has retained its doctrine of the double communion. Other Protestant denominations include the Evangelical Church of Czech Brethren.

Although many Czechs are not devout Christians in practice, Czechs in general believe in a moral upbringing for their children that will turn them into responsible citizens with a civic sense of duty. The notion of a civil

Followers of the Catholic faith taking Holy Communion outdoors.

society is close to the heart of most Czechs. They revere their first president, Tomáš Garrigue Masaryk, for his philosophical background and his ardent support for democracy and tolerance. President Václav Havel is also highly esteemed for his ideals and principles, which he incorporates into daily political life.

THE HISTORY OF JUDAISM

The presence of Jews in the Czech lands began in the 11th century, with thriving communities and businesses in Prague. In the 13th century, however, the Roman Catholic Church ordered that Jews and Christians should live separately, and Jews were moved into a walled ghetto. Jews in the Czech lands have been alternately welcomed and persecuted for several centuries—welcomed, because they were successful traders and craftsmen and paid lucrative taxes; yet persecuted by mobs and rulers alike, and forced to defend their synagogues and private property from sanctioned plunder. Under Empress Maria Theresa (1740–70), Jews were

exiled from Prague and forced to pay special taxes. Her son, Joseph II (1780–90), decreed religious tolerance because he needed more money. He ordered the ghetto walls torn down and the Jewish quarter was made a borough of Prague. It was named Josefov in his honor.

Czech Jews who survived World War II remember another ghetto, Theresienstadt (modern Terezín), which was created by the Germans as a "distribution camp" to sort the trainloads of Jews before passing them on to concentration camps. From Prague alone, 40,000 Jews made their final journey to this ghetto. Anti-Semitism was also a characteristic of the communist regime, although it was not as lethal as that promoted by Hitler.

The largest Jewish community, of 6,000, in the Czech Republic continues to be located in Josefov. There are smaller communities in Brno and Ostrava.

WHERE PEOPLE PRAY

The long history of Christianity and Judaism in the Czech Republic has resulted in beautiful and architecturally significant places of worship. Prague boasts some of the best known among them, including St. Vitus Cathedral. Located in the heart of Hradčany, the cathedral's foundation stone was laid in 1344 by Charles IV but the cathedral was not completed until 1929, when during the Czech national revival movement, a concerted effort was made to finish the work. Consequently, it is a mixture of Gothic, Renaissance, and Baroque styles. The doorways are richly decorated with carvings of historical and biblical scenes, and the interior is enhanced by traditional and modern stained-glass windows. Unfortunately, it is one of Prague's many stately and important buildings in dire need of renovation and cleaning to rid its blackened surface of the effects of ageing and pollution.

In Josefov, half a dozen original synagogues remain standing. The Old-New Synagogue is Europe's oldest synagogue. It was built in 1270 and women's prayer galleries were added in the 17th century. Some features of the synagogue that resembled symbols of Christian churches have been destroyed. Other synagogues in Josefov have been transformed to exhibit sacred Jewish artifacts, many of which were saved from demolished Bohemian synagogues. Such places dedicated to their culture and religion are of great significance to the Jews of the Czech Republic as well as to those abroad. Ironically, they were spared by Hitler from destruction so that they could form part of his "museum of an extinct race."

Above: **A statue of St. John Nepomuk was erected on Charles Bridge in 1683. It is one of the 30 statues of saints that dominate the bridge.**

Opposite: **The interior of a Jewish synagogue in Josefov.**

SUPERSTITIONS

Czechs, especially in the countryside, are superstitious. Grandparents will regale children with frightening stories that usually contain some moral or warning. One example is the story of the water man. In the Czech Republic there are many ponds and in each resides a water man. He is a terrifying figure. When young girls go to the ponds to wash their clothes, he leaps out of the water and takes them down to his lair. In his pond the water man has little pots in which he keeps the souls of the children he steals. No doubt Czech children take care around the edges of ponds and lakes.

LANGUAGE

LANGUAGE CANNOT BE SEPARATED from notions of culture, civilization, and identity. Czechs are proud of their language, which they have had to defend against foreign rulers. They see themselves as cultured and educated people, and the way they use their language reflects these beliefs.

A LANGUAGE IN THE MAKING

Most modern European, Middle Eastern, and Indian languages are derived from the family of languages called Indo-European. Czech belongs to one branch of the group, Common Slavonic.

The Slavic tribes that settled in the Czech lands had evolved a common language by the 9th century. In A.D. 863, the Byzantine monks, Cyril and Methodius, translated the Bible into the local language and the written form of Slavonic was formed.

Opposite and left: **The Czech language belongs to the West Slavonic languages, which include Polish and Slovak. Speakers of these languages have no difficulty understanding each other as their vocabulary is similar.**

In the Middle Ages, Old Church Slavonic was replaced by Latin, the language of medieval European learning. This was followed by the consolidation of German in the Bohemian kingdom, as many rulers of that period were German. The development of the Czech language was fostered by the establishment of Charles University in Prague in 1348, by the Czech king and Holy Roman emperor, Charles IV. It was the first university to be built in central Europe.

After their defeat in the Thirty Years' War (1618–48), Czechs were once again dominated by a foreign civilization. They lost their rights as citizens and German replaced the Czech language in the public affairs of the region. Czech culture and literature were stifled, but the spoken language survived in the countryside, where peasants continued to use their own language. This led to a barrier between two groups: the lower and rural classes on one side and the noble and urban classes on the other.

The government organizes classes for refugees to learn the Czech language.

In the 19th century, Josef Dobrovsky (1753–1829), a Jesuit priest and scholar, wrote a systematic grammar of the Czech language. Later, František Palacký (1798–1876), a historian and politician, published a *History of Bohemia*, a work in five volumes written in 1836–67. Both were important in establishing the Czech lands and language in the European community of nations.

In the late 19th century nationalistic sentiments took shape, and language became a crucial issue. Recognizing the need for their own cultural heritage, Czechs demanded the freedom to speak and write in their own language. They succeeded in 1918, when the independent Republic of Czechoslovakia was formed. Since then, the Czech language has not faced any real threat except during World War II, when the Nazis shut down institutes of learning. Later, under the communists, learning Russian was made compulsory in schools.

Children are taught in Czech, but they learn one major foreign language in school.

CZECH IN THE MODERN WORLD

The modern Czech language is spoken by over 10 million people. It is written in the Latin script, as is English. Above some vowels and consonants are accents that determine pronunciation.

Czech is a complex language where nouns are divided according to gender; for example, table in Czech is masculine, book is feminine, and bicycle is neuter. It is also a highly inflected language, which means the words change according to usage. For example, the ending of a noun depends on what role the noun plays in the sentence (is it the subject doing an action, or the object?) while the ending of a verb depends on its tense—present, past, or future.

FOREIGN INFLUENCES

It is inevitable that the German language continues to play a role in the Czech Republic, especially as it shares a border with Germany. Germanisms are present in the border dialects and in colloquial language. In the past, Czechs would travel to German-speaking areas in search of apprenticeships, returning fluent in German, while girls often went into service in German-speaking Austrian households. Despite racial tensions, Germans and Austrians remain Czechs' closest contact with the Western world. It is therefore expedient for Czechs, especially those in the service  industries, to speak German, and Germans are widely sought as customers and business partners.

Since the Velvet Revolution of 1989, foreign investment has been encouraged by the Czech government. There was also the widespread recognition that Czechs needed foreigners to join their companies to teach the workers new skills and knowledge. As a result, the English language has also established a foothold in the country, primarily in the major cities, in the areas of tourism and business. Many expatriate Britons, Americans, and Irish working in the cities are active in the republic's campaign to replace Russian with English as the foreign language of choice, and language schools are eager to employ native English speakers. The campaign has been successful, and language schools offering English continue to thrive.

This situation may have reached a plateau in the business world, where private companies are seen to be employing fewer foreign workers as more Czechs are now up-to-date with the knowledge and skills required. However, many advertisements in major newspapers, especially in Prague, continue to demand bilingual Czech/English speakers. Czechs have quickly come to realize the prominence of the English language in the rest of Europe. Because they were forced to learn Russian at school under the communist regime as their first foreign language, many Czechs can still speak it but choose not to.

FORMS OF ADDRESS

As every noun has a gender, surnames differ depending on whether they are male or female. The wife of a man whose surname is Navratil would be known as Navratilová. Czechs address one another with the honorary titles of *Pan* ("PAHN," Mister), *Paní* ("PA-ni," Missus), and *Slečna* ("SLE-tchna," Miss). Titles such as *doktor* and professor for teachers are also used. Forms of address combine the primary form (*Pan, Paní, Slečna*), with other titles.

Czech and Slovak are closely related linguistically, and the Czechs and Slovaks can easily understand each other.

GREETINGS

Shaking hands is customary upon meeting someone. Even people in a hurry will reach out to clasp each other's hands momentarily. Close friends also exchange kisses on both cheeks.

English is the preferred second language among secondary schoolchildren in the Czech Republic.

ARTS

THE CZECHS HAVE EXPRESSED a strong affinity for the arts throughout their history. Their buildings are magnificent examples of Gothic, Renaissance, and Baroque styles; Czech composers, writers, and dramatists have enriched the world stage; and literary and musical festivals are annual events.

THE DEVOLUTION OF DRAMA

Czech drama goes back to pre-Christian times when festivals included theatrical performances; they are still a part of the rural scene. In the 13th century plays performed in the Czech language had themes taken from daily life. By the 16th century Czech language theater had established itself, and its themes were mainly biblical. At Charles University in Prague, drama was performed in Latin and was used as a form of teaching. Some

Opposite: **The neo-Gothic church of St. Peter and Paul in Prague.**

Left: **A puppet performance of Mozart's opera,** *Don Giovanni.*

Jan Amos Comenius (1592–1670), a master scholar of his time, was born in Moravia. He wrote *Labyrinth of the World* **during the Thirty Years' War. He was exiled along with other Protestant scholars by an imperial edict of 1627, and never returned to his homeland.**

plays, known as *schola ludus,* or school games, were written by Jan Amos Comenius in the 17th century. After the Thirty Years' War, the Czech language theater vanished, reappearing only more than a century later, in Prague.

The First Czechoslovak Republic saw much experimentation in theater. In contrast, the communist period after World War II saw the production of good classical theater, but hardly any modern productions. Plays produced by dissident playwrights such as Václav Havel were banned because of their anti-government slant. The Western world gained access to them, so the work of the dissidents became known outside their own country. The mid to late 1960s provided a respite from government censorship, and consequently free expression was explored in Prague's theaters such as the Theater by the Railings, which was founded in 1958.

Since the overthrow of communism, new theater groups have appeared. The drama festival called Island Theater, begun in 1985, is held every year and includes an arts and crafts fair. Theater is a passion for many Czechs, especially the elderly. Under the communist regime the arts were subsidized and theaters were full. Ticket prices have since increased but are still affordable with concessions.

PUPPET THEATER Marionette plays have been popular since the 16th century, their popularity peaking in the 17th and early 18th centuries. They were considered children's entertainment until a revival in the 20th century. Josef Skupa's legendary puppets, Špejbel and Hurvínek, created in the 1920s, still perform in Prague.

NATURALLY MUSICAL

Czechs have a common saying: "Scratch a Czech, find a musician underneath." The Arab explorer Ibrahim ibn Jakub described string and woodwind instruments used by the Slavs in the region of Bohemia in A.D. 965. An 11th or 12th century lute is the earliest instrument found in that region. Four 14th century hymns in the Czech language have also been discovered.

The 15th century Hussite movement was responsible for the creation of distinctive Czech hymns. Folk music developed swiftly after that, and is still enjoyed in villages today. This growth was followed by a period of stagnation when Czech music survived only at the village level, or was kept alive by Czech emigrants, such as Jan Dismas Zelenka, who worked in Dresden in the 18th century.

The 19th century was a rich and productive time. Bedřich Smetana (1824–84), believed to be the first nationalist Czech composer, departed from traditional melodies in composing his operas and symphonic poems. His best-known works include *The Brandenburgers in Bohemia* and *The Bartered Bride*. He lost his hearing in 1874. Over the next five years he wrote a cycle of six symphonic poems, collectively called *Ma Vlast* (My Country), about Bohemia. In listening to one of them, *Vltava (The Moldau)*, the listener follows the course of the river beside which Smetana spent many hours arranging his compositions.

While Smetana laid the foundation of nationalist music, Antonín Dvořák (1841–1904), second viola in Smetana's orchestra, developed this theme and left an abundant heritage—31 works of chamber music, 14 string quartets, 50 orchestral works, and nine symphonies. Dvořák started

Bedřich Smetana, the Czechs' favorite composer, resigned as conductor at the National Theater in Prague in 1874 because of his deafness. He died insane and poor ten years later.

his musical career playing the violin in his father's inn and paid his way through a two-year music course in Prague. In 1875 he met the German composer Johannes Brahms, whose friendship and patronage led to the publication of Dvořák's *Moravian Duets* (1876) and *Slavonic Dances* (1878). Dvořák achieved fame in England for his choral music and was made director of the National Conservatory of Music in New York in 1892; the three years he spent in New York resulted in his *Symphony No. 9 From the New World*. Despite his fame abroad, he remained a humble, religious family man, who was most at home in the Bohemian countryside.

Leoš Janáček (1854–1928), another nationalist composer who was a contemporary of Smetana and Dvořák, was born in Moravia. He founded a college of organists in Brno in 1881, and was its director for almost 40 years. Janáček composed choral music as well as chamber and orchestral works, and much of his work is based on traditional folk music. He was particularly skilled in manipulating the music for dramatic effect. Among his internationally famous operas are *The Cunning Little Vixen* and *From the House of the Dead*. *Kat'a Kabanová* is an opera that resulted from his interest in Russian language and literature.

ARTISANS OF BOHEMIA Early 18th century Bohemia was known as the conservatory of Europe, as increasingly Bohemian artists and composers were establishing themselves all over Europe. This musical heritage is partly founded on the Bohemian tradition of making lutes and violins.

Lute-making preceded violin-making by several centuries. Plucked instruments predominated because, until the early 17th century, singing rather than instrumental music was the fashion, and it was easier to sing to a lute than to a bowed instrument. The use of lutes dates back to at least the 13th century, and the lute is illustrated in Jan Amos Comenius's *Orbis Sensualium Pictus* (The World in Pictures).

Many Bohemian Protestants emigrated to other German-speaking lands to avoid the forced Catholicization of their country after 1620. Once settled, they established some of the earliest craft guilds ever recorded. Ironically, the religious and political changes wrought by the devastation of the Thirty Years' War provided the impetus to the development of music in general. The Church established closer ties with the populace and provided grand churches and religious ceremonies for which musicians could compose music. In this setting, the string instruments found their niche. This period, the Baroque, was a high point in musical development.

The latter half of the 17th century saw many immigrants from Germany and Tyrol. This infusion of knowledge and skill in making violins provided an impetus to the local artisans. Typically, a master of the craft would open up a shop. His sons would be introduced to the craft from an early age, learning as apprentices, and would continue the family tradition. Guilds were established, and most artisans established themselves in Prague.

Violin playing is one of the oldest skills in the Czech lands. One of Bohemia's most famous 19th century composers, Antonín Dvořák, began his musical career fiddling in his father's inn. The violin makers were usually skilled players.

During the national revival movement (late 18th and 19th centuries), Czech craftsmen began to leave Prague to work in smaller towns. The humble beginnings of a group of people who were to become Czech masters appeared in a small town called Paseky, in the hills dividing northern Bohemia from German Silesia. Venceslav Metelka, a joiner and self-taught violin maker, trained his sons and daughter in the trade. A school established itself over time, with more family members becoming artisans and taking on pupils. This family is but one example of a long-standing tradition of musical artisanship that became part of the national psyche. The Czechs can claim that musical prowess runs in their veins.

The violins made varied in the shape and curve of the instrument, the type of wood used, the size and angles of the holes, the quality of the acoustics, and the color of the wood varnish. Many violin makers placed labels with their names on their products, although often the name of the shop owner rather than the apprentice would appear on the finished item. Many of these men were musicians as well, and had a deep affinity with their craft. At about this time, too, the working class began to develop an interest in cultural pursuits, and many locally made violins found their way into middle-class homes.

FOLK ARTS AND CRAFTS

Much of the physical evidence of folk traditions reaches back only to the 19th century national revival, due to the perishable nature of most materials. Folk arts take the forms of stories, songs, music, dance, clothing, and architectural styles. These traditions have been preserved to this day in families, passing from each generation to a younger one, or publicly, through museums and festivals. Folk festivals usually occur in the summer or autumn, and provide the focus for neighbors to gather and enjoy themselves with music and dancing, and wearing traditional folk dress. The sleepy town of Strážnice, for example, suddenly comes to life at the end of June for the International Folklore Festival. Participants from all over Europe take part in competitions.

FOLK MUSEUMS All over the countryside are open-air museums called *skansens* that house traditional architecture and furnishings. Some are sites of folk festivals, and the better ones attempt to show not only single buildings but the way entire communities lived. For this purpose, barns, churches, and other buildings have been transported piece by piece and filled with utensils, linen, and clothing typical of the period.

Above: **Folk dancers show off the vibrant colors of their traditional dress.**

Opposite: **An open-air folk museum, or** *skansen.*

BOHEMIAN CRYSTAL

As legend has it, an old woman was walking through the Giant Mountains carrying a basket of newly made glassware to market when she slipped and fell, smashing her goods to pieces. Devastated though she was, she listened to Krakono, the spirit of the mountains, who commanded her to take her basket of shattered glass home. Upon her arrival, she found that the broken glass had been transformed into gold.

Czechs, especially Bohemians, have been discovering gold in the trade of cut and engraved glass and crystal for several centuries. In the latter half of the 17th century, the small trade of glass cutting and engraving established itself formally into guilds. As interest in decorated glass grew, Bohemian craftsmen developed a rock crystal type of glass, which expanded the range of decoration possible. Limestone was the key ingredient in this glass, giving it greater brilliance and providing a more striking contrast with the matt engraving. By the end of the 17th century the knowledge of how to make limestone crystal glass had spread throughout Bohemia and reached other parts of Europe. Bohemian glass began to be exported, and by the end of the 18th century had reached most of Europe, the Middle East, and the Americas. Engravers took inspiration from many sources—biblical tales, images from coins and maps, and the landscape around them. Bohemian artisans also traveled widely with their wares and customized their products to buyers' requests.

Glass and crystal continue to be produced in Bohemia today. As with most crafts that began before the industrial revolution, glass cutting and engraving have become an industry based on mass production. The days of only the nobility being able to afford such beautiful objects are gone. Engraved glass and crystal are now affordable commodities.

BETWEEN BLACK AND WHITE

In the 20th century photography as an art form took root in the Czech lands. An artist in this field was Josef Sudek (1896–1976), who was apprenticed at the age of 15 to a bookbinder. A fellow worker introduced him to amateur photography, and after losing his right arm fighting in World War I, he decided to become a photographer. He studied photography at the School of Graphic Art for two years. He absorbed influences from past and contemporary painting traditions, and in time he came to express a unique, romantic style, concentrating on gradations of tone. One of his most striking series is of St. Vitus Cathedral in Prague—over 100 photographs juxtaposing the grand building with the prosaic detail of construction materials. Sudek dedicated himself to photographing his country, especially Prague. Many exhibitions of his work were held during his lifetime, in his country and abroad, especially in New York City. In his later years he worked to earn just enough money for his expenses, preferring to concentrate on his creative visions. He said, "You should never lose contact with that which is close to your heart; at the most you can make an interruption for half a year. If it is longer, you lose the thread and never find it again."

One of Franz Kafka's homes in Prague. Kafka's relatively short life was spent mostly in the capital, where he worked as a legal clerk for 14 years, writing after work. Many of his manuscripts were confiscated by the German secret police in 1931, and have never been found.

LITERATURE

The earliest Czech literary works were hymns and religious texts in Old Church Slavonic and 10th century legends of St. Wenceslas. Jan Hus's *Orthographia Bohemica* was among the religious tracts of the 14th century. Themes of morality and chronicles of daily life and journeys were featured in 16th and 17th century prose. The persecution of scholars since the 17th century discouraged local creative writing for about two centuries.

From the mid-19th to the early 20th centuries, writing assumed nationalistic and political themes. Among writers of this period are Jaroslav Hašek (1883–1924) and Karel Čapek (1890–1938). Hašek, a practical joker, had a colorful career—he was, in turn, bank clerk, newspaper editor (by age 21), soldier in World War I, prisoner of war of the Russians, and communist propagandist for the Bolsheviks, before turning to writing full-time. His novels made fun of authoritarian regimes, and he is best known for *The Good Soldier Schweyk*, a satire on military life. Čapek, a Czech novelist, playwright, and essayist, explored morality in his works. He often collaborated with his brother Josef, a dramatist and illustrator, in writing plays.

In the same period, Jan Neruda (1834–91) wrote popular light fiction about 19th century Prague. Two famous collections of his are *Tales of the Lesser Quarter* and *Pictures of Old Prague*.

There was a strong tradition of writing in German. An Austrian group known as the Prague Circle included Jewish fiction writer Franz Kafka (1883–1924), novelist, poet, and playwright Franz Werfel (1890–1945), and the poet Rainer Maria Rilke (1875–1926). When World War II ended, the German minority was expelled, and this tradition ended.

MILAN KUNDERA

Milan Kundera was born on April 1, 1929, in Brno. He studied filmmaking at the Academy of Music and Dramatic Arts in Prague (FAMU) and focused on writing films and directing. In 1954 he became a lecturer in literature at FAMU where he taught until 1969. Meanwhile, he gained prominence for his work in poetry, drama, film, and prose fiction. His first novel, *The Joke*, and a collection of stories, *Laughable Loves*, were published in Prague before 1968. *The Joke* was translated into more than 20 languages and brought him international recognition. After the Warsaw Pact invasion of Czechoslovakia, Kundera was marked as a dissident by the communist government. He moved to France where he taught comparative literature. In 1979, in response to the publication of his novel *The Book of Laughter and Forgetting*, the Czechoslovak government revoked his Czech citizenship. Two years later, he became a naturalized French citizen.

Kundera's literary awards include the Czechoslovak Writers Publishing House Prize for his critical study of novelist Vladislav Vancura in *Art of the Novel* (1961) and for *Laughable Loves* (1969); the Klement Lukes Prize (1963) for his play *The Owners of the Keys;* the Czechoslovak Writers Union Prize (1968) for *The Joke;* the French Prix Médicis (1973) for *Life is Elsewhere;* the Italian Premio Letterario Mondello (1978) for *The Farewell Waltz;* the American Commonwealth Award and the Prix Europa-Littérature in recognition of his contribution to literature; and the Los Angeles Times Prize in 1984 for *The Unbearable Lightness of Being*, which was made into a film.

Communism dampened the literary spirit; the 1950s saw writing in the social realism style. The Prague Spring of the 1960s saw a flowering of writing, with authors such as Milan Kundera. After the invasion of Warsaw Pact troops in 1968, he was among the writers who were forced to leave the country in order to continue their work.

POETIC TENDENCIES Czech poetry is not popularly read in other countries because it is difficult to translate and interpret. Karel Hynek Mácha (1810–36) is considered the greatest 19th century Czech poet. He was greatly influenced by English and Polish Romantic literature, and his lyrical epic *May* has been highly praised by 20th century poets and critics. Mácha died of pneumonia just before his 26th birthday.

Jaroslav Seifert (1901–86) was a journalist until 1950, then a freelance writer. His poetry reflects the momentous events of the German occupation of Czechoslovakia, the Soviet coup of 1948, and the liberation of the Prague Spring. His themes range from patriotism to political critiques. His work began to be republished in the Czech Republic in 1979. Seifert won the Nobel Prize in Literature in 1984.

In 1985 Milan Kundera received the Jerusalem Prize, awarded every two years to "the writer who has contributed most to the world's understanding of the freedom of the individual in society." But Czechs are ambivalent towards him, feeling he is no longer "Czech" as he now writes in French.

PAINTING

Early examples of painting in the Czech lands include illuminated manuscripts and church frescoes of the Romanesque period and Byzantine paintings in the late 13th century. Book illumination was the dominant form of painting during the late Gothic and Renaissance periods.

Czech realism flowered during the later stages of the revival movement in the 19th century when subject matter dealt with the prosaic. An era of landscape art was followed by Impressionism and Symbolism.

Art Nouveau became very popular in the late 19th and early 20th centuries. Many Czech artists were inspired by the Art Nouveau styles of Paris. Among them was Alfons Mucha (1860–1939), famed for his delicate female figures whose hair and clothes merged with the background in elaborate, decorative detail. He achieved fame for his posters advertising French actress Sarah Bernhardt in her many roles. In his later travels to the United States, he met Chicago industrialist Charles Richard Crane, who sponsored 20 large historical paintings in the series "Epic of the Slavic People," which were completed between 1912 and 1930.

Surrealism inspired Czech artists in the early 20th century and continues to be influential. For artists like Eva Svankmajerova, the focus of surrealism is the freedom of the individual, which continues to be highly relevant.

ARCHITECTURE

The earliest buildings in Bohemia and Moravia were made of wood. The oldest surviving buildings are built in Romanesque style with thick walls, rounded arches, and large, closely spaced columns. From the 13th to 16th centuries, the Gothic style dominated the Czech lands. Individual buildings as well as town squares surrounded by arcaded houses built in that period still stand today.

Fanciful facades dominate the Old Town Square in Prague.

In the early 16th century Italian Renaissance style developed distinct Czech touches, including stucco decorations of historical scenes. The Baroque style of the early 18th century can be seen throughout the country. Its distinctive features include grand sculptures and frescoes, and gilded ornamentation. In the 19th century there was a revival of old architectural styles—neo-classical, neo-Gothic, and neo-Renaissance. Many beautiful hotels and cafés in Prague speak evocatively of this period. The communist era stifled creativity, leaving a legacy of ugly, massive, concrete public buildings and prefabricated housing villages.

Many architectural treasures are in need of restoration, and the government has set aside funds for their conservation.

CINEMA

The Czech film industry in the early 20th century produced mainly silent comedies. The Nazi occupiers restricted film production to nationalistic comedies, and the communist regime that followed allowed only low quality propaganda films. The number of films made after World War II declined. Nevertheless Karel Steklí's *Siren* (1947) was awarded the Golden Lion in Venice. In 1949, 12-year-old Ivan Jandl was the first Czech awarded an Oscar, for a role in a film by Fred Zinnemann.

Despite tense political conditions in the 1950s, Czech films attained some success abroad. In 1958, Karel Zeman's *The Invention of Destruction* was awarded the Expo 58 Grand Prix in Brussels and Weis's *The Wolves' Hole* won the FIPRESCI Award in Venice.

Young Czech directors escaped censorship because, as the first graduates of the Academy of Film under communist rule, they were assumed to be ideologically clean. The director Miloš Forman began his career during this period but fled after the Warsaw Pact invasion in 1968.

Miloš Forman receiving a Golden Globe award in 1997 for The People vs. Larry Flynt. Forman also directed *One Flew Over The Cuckoo's Nest*, and *Amadeus*. The latter was largely filmed in Prague.

LEISURE

CZECHS PURSUE a variety of activities for enjoyment, from traditional sports to pastimes such as gathering mushrooms and berry-picking, or simply spending the weekend at their country cottage.

THE SOKOL MOVEMENT

Physical education has a long tradition in the republic. A Czech professor of art history at Charles University, Miroslav Tyrš (1832–84), founded an exercise movement called Sokol in 1862, convinced that citizens needed to be of healthy mind and body in order to survive as a nation. Although the movement was based on a tradition of physical education stretching back to Renaissance times, its role was essentially a political one, to inspire nationalistic pride in the people at a time when they were struggling for independence.

Part of the Sokol tradition involved rallies where thousands of people would exercise in formation in a stadium, using banners and ribbons for a striking display. Sokol members were targeted by the Nazis during the German occupation of Czechoslovakia in World War II and by the communists after the war, but Czechs held on to the tradition, fulfilling Miroslav Tyrš' purpose of promoting nationalism. Sokol was revived publicly after 1989, and in 1994 a Sokol rally in the summer attracted large crowds.

SPORTS

Czechs have great enthusiasm for many modern sports. Soccer is a national passion and the country is always represented in the European soccer championship matches. Czechs also enjoy a national soccer competition.

Above: **Young and old enjoying Sokol practice.**

Opposite: **Waiting for the midday meal to be cooked while on a camping holiday by Rožmberk Lake.**

Second to soccer as a national sport is ice hockey. Czechs have participated in European and world championships since the end of the 19th century. Ice skating is also a favorite pastime. During the winter, when temperatures fall below freezing, sections of some parks are sprayed with water and turned into ice rinks. Czechs also like to ski, and given the mountainous terrain of the country, there is a wide choice of slopes.

Tennis has an enthusiastic following. The Skoda Czech Open is held in early August in Prague. Famous Czech tennis players include Martina Navratilová and Ivan Lendl. Both are now United States citizens.

Another favorite pastime is cycling in the countryside. The Czech landscape provides many varied and stunning locations, from the foothills of mountain ranges to the lakes in South Bohemia. Not many people cycle in the larger cities because of the predominance of cobbled streets, heavy traffic, and air pollution.

The Prague Marathon inaugurated in 1989 has become an annual event, although more foreigners than Czechs take part in it. It is held at the end of June and is followed by late night partying in Prague.

A COUNTRY RETREAT

On the weekends, Czech families head for their country cottages. The notion of a country retreat is a long-standing one in Czech culture. These second homes may be ancestral cottages passed down through the family, cottages left vacant by people who moved to the cities, or newly built chalets on the edge of villages.

After World War II, about three million Germans were forced to leave the Czech lands and return to Germany, abandoning their property. Czechs moved into the empty homes, and possessed them by the simple process of occupying the buildings. During the communist years, when citizens were not allowed to express thoughts or beliefs contrary to the approved government policy, these second homes became a place of retreat for many people.

In the communist era the country cottages were often in a state of extreme disrepair. More recently, people have begun to spend money renovating and restoring these properties. Czechs proudly refer to their "golden hands," saying they are naturally adept at completing any manual task. Many spend the work week planning what renovations and repairs they will complete on the weekend, and their efforts during the work week are spent on getting the right equipment.

The 1997 floods devastated many country homes. It will take time to repair the damage or rebuild the destroyed homes. It is almost certain though that the country cottage will continue as a Czech tradition.

In the late summer and early autumn many people spend their weekends at their country cottage picking mushrooms. Some people concentrate on only one or two species, while others may collect dozens of different fungi. There are many ways to preserve them, and a lot of time is spent in the kitchen drying, pickling, and freezing the mushrooms for later use.

Left: **Czechs who can afford it have country homes where they live on weekends and over the long summer vacation.**

Opposite: **Winters bring excellent tobogganing weather—there are between 40 and 130 days of snowfall in the republic.**

Visitors to the spa in Karlovy Vary (Carlsbad) drinking the spa water.

FREE TO TRAVEL

Recently, Czechs have become great travelers abroad. During the four decades under a communist regime, travel was not allowed. Once the restrictions were lifted, travel became a desired and planned-for pastime. The cheaper holiday destinations in Europe such as Croatia and Spain are very popular.

Czechs are used to being self-sufficient because of limited funds. They tend to travel by bus as it is cheaper, and usually take their own food with them while on vacation. This makes them unpopular in other countries, as they do not spend as much money as other tourists!

Their recent passion for travel has had one unfortunate result—the burgeoning of travel agencies without the institution of adequate regulations to guide them. In 1997, over 11 Czech travel companies failed, leaving travelers stranded in distant locations such as Sudan, and Czech missions abroad were forced to help stranded travelers return home.

HEALING WATERS

The republic has many naturally occurring mineral springs, particularly in West Bohemia and North Moravia. Spa towns have developed where people go to treat their medical conditions, usually by bathing in the waters or drinking it. West Bohemia spa towns include Karlovy Vary, Jáchymov, Františkovy Lázně, and Mariánské Lázně; in North Moravia a number of spa towns are located near the Jeseníky Mountains.

The spas specialize in treating one or more ailments—respiratory, thyroid, coronary, and rheumatic diseases; allergies; diseases of the liver, kidney, stomach, and skin; and gynecological complaints are some of them. Famous people have convalesced at the spas, and elderly Czechs especially enjoy taking the baths, whether to treat specific ailments or simply because they like reclining in thermal waters. Most spa towns are located amid magnificent countryside.

PARKS AND THE ARTS

Larger towns and cities will usually have one or several public parks, and some feature formal gardens with carefully trimmed shrubs bordering arcaded walks. Czechs of all ages take advantage of these stretches of green for strolls, picnics, or a leisurely read under the magnolia trees. In the summer, the parks are filled with people throwing frisbees, playing guitars, or walking their dogs.

A favorite leisure activity for older Czechs is the theater, especially opera. The arts have remained a constant factor in the lives of all Czechs. Those who have the time like to attend the many festivals and concerts offered in the larger cities. The concerts are not as accessible as they once were (under the communist regime, tickets were subsidized) but retired citizens are still entitled to lower ticket prices.

Since Karlovy Vary was founded by Charles IV in the 14th century, other famous people have "taken the waters" at the spa towns in the Czech lands. Among them are German poet and dramatist Johann Wolfgang von Goethe, composer Johann Sebastian Bach, and socialist philosopher Karl Marx.

FESTIVALS

CZECH FESTIVALS ARE A GLORIOUS MIXTURE of Christian and pre-Christian rituals. Throughout the country, rites celebrating the seasons are held, varying in detail according to the region. Added to those are festivals of cultural and nationalistic significance to Czechs. Many of the festivals are celebrated in both the cities and the rural towns, while some are unique to certain locations. In addition to festivals celebrated by all, nearly every day of the year is the day of a saint. A name day (the day of the saint after whom one is named) is as important as a birthday. Newspapers publish lists of saints' days, and these help people to remember friends' name days with small gifts or cards.

Above: **Decorated Easter eggs hanging from their ribbons for sale.**

Opposite: **Rider in a festival procession.**

CHRISTIAN TRADITIONS

Under the communist regime, the holy days of Easter and Christmas were work holidays, and their religious significance was played down by the government.

EASTER The religious celebrations of Easter are integrated with pre-Christian rituals marking the change of seasons. The end of fasting on Palm Sunday is also a celebration of the arrival of spring. The figure of Death, made from sticks and cloth, is ceremoniously burned, representing the end of winter. Traditional Czechs decorate green branches with bright ribbons and eggs, symbolizing the cycle of new life, and bathe in springs believed to have a rejuvenating effect. In another Easter custom, beautifully decorated eggs are placed in house and shop windows. People also place other symbols of new life in the windows, such as pussy willow and dolls

107

Street entertainers perform in Prague over the Christmas season.

made of straw. Moravians especially decorate their houses with floral designs, using soap on windows or sand in backyards.

One spring ritual connected with Easter persists throughout the countryside: men and boys go around gently swatting women and girls with willow switches. In some places the women respond with buckets of water and in others with Easter eggs. This is meant to represent rejuvenation, and it involves much merriment.

CHRISTMAS is a time for gifts, fun, and feasting, as it is elsewhere. Although their religious significance has dimmed considerably, the rituals associated with Christmas continue to be enjoyed by many Czechs.

On St. Nicholas' Day, December 5, St. Nicholas and the Devil visit the homes of family and close friends. They are usually someone's father and uncle dressed up. St. Nicholas looks remarkably like the Catholic Pope in a tall, white hat and long, white coat, and carries a staff. The Devil wears a mask or heavy black make-up, horns on his head, an old fur coat, and sometimes a tail and a chain that rattles as he walks. Children who have been good receive a small gift such as fruit, nuts, or chocolate, whereas children who have been bad are given a piece of coal.

Christmas Eve is also called Generous Day, and is special for its gift-giving and big family meals. Dinner begins with carp soup, followed by either carp fried with breadcrumbs and served with potato salad or carp in black sauce. Dessert is a light fruitcake. Presents are opened with much enthusiasm after dinner, and some people still like to go to midnight Mass.

Christmas Day is a family event. Lunch is traditionally roast turkey, dumplings, and sauerkraut. Most families participate in fun activities such as bobbing for apples. The next day, St. Stephen's Day, is spent recuperating. The Christmas season ends on January 6, the Day of the Three Kings, which is sometimes marked by carols and bell-ringing.

BURNING OF THE WITCHES

This festival, celebrated on April 30, represents a pre-Christian ritual to ward off evil forces. Witches were a special target, for they were believed to ride off on broomsticks to meet with the Devil.

Today the occasion is used to mark the end of winter, and involves night parties around bonfires. There are romantic customs for young couples—they jump over dying embers together, and the next day men leave branches with new leaves on the doorstep of their favorite girl.

In the Burning of the Witches ceremony, peasants tidied their properties and gathered on the highest hill for a grand burning of their brooms as a defense against the witches.

In December, live carp—traditional Christmas fare for Czechs—is sold on the streets of Prague.

NATIONAL HOLIDAYS

January 1 — *Nový rok*, or New Year's Day, is also the anniversary of the creation of the Czech Republic in 1993.

March or April — *Pondělí velikonočni*, or Easter Monday.

May 1 — *Svátek práce*, Labor Day, was very significant under the communist regime; it is now a day of enjoyment, usually spent picnicking in the countryside, and often preceded by all-night revels.

May 5 — *Den osvobozeni* is Liberation Day, when Czechs commemorate the liberation of Prague from Nazi occupiers in 1945.

July 5 — *Den Cyrila a Metoděje*, the Saints' Day for Cyril and Methodius, celebrates the introduction of Christianity to Slavs and the beginning of their written language.

July 6 — *Den Jana Husa*, or Jan Hus Day, commemorates the burning at the stake in 1415 of the great theologian and religious reformer.

October 28 — *Den vzniku Československa* is Independence Day, the anniversary of the founding of the First Czechoslovak Republic in 1918.

December 24–26 — *Vánoce*, the Christmas holiday.

COMMEMORATIVE DATES

January 19   Anniversary of the death of Jan Palach, the Charles University student who immolated himself in 1969 in protest against the Soviet occupation of his country. Czechs offer flowers in Wenceslas Square to mark this day (picture below).

March 7   Birthday of Tomáš Garrigue Masaryk, Czechoslovakia's much-revered first president.

May 5   *České povstání*, the anniversary of the anti-Nazi uprising by the people of Prague. The fierce fighting began on May 5, 1945 and lasted four days.

July   A mock battle (see picture opposite) commemorates the decisive Battle of Chlum on July 3, 1866, when 221,000 Prussians defeated 215,000 Austrian and Saxon troops, leaving 53,000 dead, only 9,000 of whom were Prussian. Over 460 graves and tombstones mark the battlefield. Every July, memorials are held in this little North Bohemian town. Chlum was made a commemorative zone in 1996.

November 17   International Students' Day, known as the "day of students' fight for freedom and democracy." This is the anniversary of the closure of Czech universities by the Germans in 1939; it also commemorates the student demonstrations that led to the collapse of the communist government in 1989.

CULTURAL EVENTS

Mid-May   Prague International Book Fair

May 12–June 4   *Pražské Jaro*

     Prague Spring International Music Festival

July   Karlovy Vary Film Festival

September   Prague Mozart Festival

FESTIVALS

April 30   *Pálení čarodějnic*, Burning of the Witches

May   Ride of the Kings

June   International Folklore Festival, Strážnice

December 5   St. Nicholas' Day

Folk singers and dancers in full costume put on a show for the crowds in Strážnice every June.

THE STRÁŽNICE INTERNATIONAL FOLKLORE FESTIVAL

Since it was first held in 1945, the International Folklore Festival in Strážnice, Moravia, has played a key role in the preservation of traditional dress, music, and dance. National customs survived during communist rule even without socialist subsidies.

The festivities take place over two days in the park of a castle, with both organized and impromptu musical performances, food stalls, and plenty of beer and wine. Festival highlights include a procession of people in costumes from all over Europe, which starts at the town's main square and makes it way to the castle park. Festivities continue into the night. Open-air shows are enjoyed by children and adults alike.

RIDE OF THE KINGS

On the last weekend of May, a few remaining towns in southeast Moravia continue the tradition of the Ride of the Kings. The festival celebrates the spring's new crops and the ride itself relates to a young man's rite of passage, believed to hark back to an older European festival. Celebrating spring and new growth involves a lot of feasting accompanied by music and dancing. Intricately decorated folk dress is worn as part of the singing and dancing events.

For two days, the "king" recruits his helpers, then on Sunday they ride around town together to be accepted by the adult men. The king must be chaste, so he is usually about 12 years old. His helpers can be up to 18 years old.

The king holds a rose clenched between his teeth throughout the ceremony as he is not permitted to smile. He and his helpers are dressed in women's clothing, which is part of an ancient ritual to protect the crops. The horses are decorated with ribbons and paper flowers. The ride begins at the home of the king and winds its way through the village. Along the way, the helpers call out in verse for gifts for the king, and bystanders respond by placing money in the helpers' boots. The celebrations end with a parade, and more singing and dancing.

Autumn is a time of local festivals associated with the harvest. On such occasions, a pig may be roasted to celebrate the year's crop or vintage.

Many Czech festivals are related to the seasons. Here, a procession marks a harvest festival in the autumn.

FOOD

OVER THE CENTURIES, Czech cuisine has absorbed Austrian, Hungarian, German, and Polish influences. The traditional Hungarian goulash and German sauerkraut have become Czech staples. Czechs enjoy the Slavic custom of flavoring foods with sour cream, lemon, vinegar, and green grapes.

TRADITIONAL FARE

A typical Czech meal includes lots of meat and big portions of dumplings, potatoes, or rice covered in a thick sauce, accompanied by cooked vegetables or sauerkraut. Czechs are big meat eaters who prefer pork. Poultry is roasted, whether chicken or the favorite—farm-bred goose. The roast is served with the ever-present dumplings and sauerkraut.

Above: **A typical Czech meal of pork served with pickles.**

Opposite: **An outdoor café, one of many in Prague.**

Czechs also enjoy preserved or pickled vegetables. Fresh vegetables, with the exception of salads, are not a regular part of a Czech meal. Bacon, caraway seeds, and salt are typical flavorings. In the autumn Czechs greatly enjoy the bountiful supply of a variety of mushrooms, which they pick on trips to the countryside.

As the republic is a landlocked country, seafood is generally not present on the dining table. However, trout fished from mountain streams is enjoyed by Czechs, as is carp from the ponds in South Bohemia. A meal with carp as the main dish is the traditional fare at Christmas.

Bread is made in many styles, although rye bread is by far the most common, often flavored with caraway seeds.

Snacks can consist of smoked meats or thick, spicy pork or beef sausages, which may be fried or boiled. The sausages are often served with mustard on rye bread or a wheat roll. Patties made from strips of raw potato and garlic are also a typical snack. Rye and wheat bread will often be served with cold meats and cheeses.

Breakfast typically consists of bread with butter, cheese, eggs, ham or sausage, jam or yogurt, and tea or coffee. Workers hurrying off to work may stop at a small café, often equipped with a narrow counter or small, tall tables, around which customers stand to hurriedly consume soup, rolls, and sausages. Some Czechs bring sandwiches to work, to eat during their 10 a.m. break. Lunch is the main meal, but is usually a hurried affair, except on Sundays. If people can afford it, they go out for lunch and are always happy to enjoy a long break. Dinner will be a light meal and may consist of a cold buffet of meats and cheese with bread.

The kitchen is still very much a woman's domain. Many women prefer that their husbands stay out of the kitchen and think nothing of spending several hours preparing the main meal without help. For a husband to wash the dishes is an odd occurrence in most homes.

A typical main meal usually begins with soup. It may be a broth with pieces of bacon, vegetables, or noodles, or a thick and heavy soup, such as potato with vegetables and mushrooms, sliced tripe with spices, or thick spicy beef and potato soup. The main course often consists of dumplings, sauerkraut, and roast pork chops or goose. Another very common main course is roast beef and goulash, served with a dill cream sauce or mushroom sauce. A Czech speciality is roast beef served with lemon, cranberries, and bread dumplings in a sour cream sauce. French fries or rice may accompany the main course. Beer, rather than imported soft drinks, usually accompanies every course of a meal.

Topping the pastry with cream and fruit preserve.

DUMPLINGS AND OTHER DESSERTS

Dumplings are a common part of Czech cuisine. They accompany most main meals but are also made in sweet versions for dessert. Typical savory dumplings are made with either a bread or potato base. *Kynute knedliky* (raised dumplings), which is made from milk, eggs, and yeast, rises like bread. A traditional part of Christmas lunch is bread or liver dumplings, the latter flavored with lemon rind and marjoram. A very common sweet dumpling is plum dumpling, where dried plums or prunes are wrapped in a thin layer of dough, boiled, and then rolled in crushed poppyseeds mixed with cinnamon sugar. Fruit dumplings are a summer speciality, not only plum but also blueberry and apricot, dripping with melted butter and served with cottage cheese.

Another favorite dessert for adults and children alike is *vanilkove roblicky*. This crescent-shaped sweet, flavored with vanilla and almonds and dusted with icing sugar, is served especially at Christmas.

Dumplings are served with almost every meal.

After a serious operation and many days in intensive care, vanilla crescents were the first food President Václav Havel chose to eat.

117

WHAT TO DRINK

A Czech will usually offer a guest Turkish-style coffee. Hot water is poured over ground beans that end up as sludge at the bottom of the cup. Tea, which is not as common, is usually served with lemon. On a hot day, beer is offered. Few Czechs drink tap water. This custom was reinforced after the winter floods of 1997, which saw the contamination of many drinking water supplies.

Although Czechs are great beer consumers, Moravia is well-known as a wine-growing region, especially in the southeast. A favorite pastime for friends and family is to gather at family-run wine cellars to taste wine and sing. A drink often enjoyed in the summer is white wine and soda on ice. Czechs prefer hot wine in the winter.

Moravia is also famous for its fiery brandies, both plum and apricot as well as cherry liqueurs. A popular drink all year round is a mixture of rum and hot water in equal parts, flavored with lemon. The spa town of Karlovy Vary jealously guards the recipe to its locally produced spicy herbal liqueur, which is often served as an aperitif.

Czechs enjoy sipping the local wine when dining out, although their all-time favorite drink is beer.

FAMOUS BEER DRINKERS Beer drinkers have a choice of a variety of good beers, especially in Prague, for the home of Czech beer is Bohemia. The earliest record of the brewing tradition in Prague is a document dated 1082, while the famous beer town of Plzeň (Pilsen) was allowed to produce its own beer in 1290. Czechs drink 34 gallons (154 liters) per capita each year—equivalent to more than 300 pint glasses of beer.

In Bohemia, beer accompanies most meals, including breakfast. Czechs drink beer the way Americans drink soft drinks. Beer is served almost everywhere, except in the wine bars. Most Czech beers are lagers, naturally brewed from hand-picked hops, and containing between 3% and 6% alcohol. People like to drink their beer cold with a creamy head. Beer is known as *pivo* in all Slavonic languages.

Czech beers such as Budvar and Pilsener Urquell are well-known throughout the world. Budvar, the original Budweiser beer, is exported to 21 countries. One of Bohemia's oldest beers is the brand Regent, which has been in production since 1379. Bohemian beers are believed to be the best in the world because of the superior quality of Bohemian hops.

Beer, is produced by heating ground malt with water and hops before allowing the mixture to ferment at low temperatures by the addition of a special yeast.

Eating outdoors is a popular summer pursuit for Czechs.

SVESTKOVE KNEDLIKY (PLUM DUMPLINGS)

4 tablespoons butter	2 cups boiled potatoes, riced
2 eggs	12–15 pitted prunes
pinch of salt	$1/4$ cup cinnamon sugar
2 cups sifted all-purpose flour	1 cup fine breadcrumbs

Cream 2 tablespoons butter, and beat in eggs and salt. Gradually beat in the flour and potatoes. The dough should be stiff so it can be kneaded well.

On a floured board, roll out the dough until it is $1/4$ inch (5 mm) thick. Cut it into 3 inch (7 cm) squares. Place a prune on each square, sprinkle with the sugar, and fold the edges over the plum. Form a square with each one.

Place the dumplings into a pot of boiling water, cover, and simmer for 15 minutes. Melt the remaining butter in a pan and brown the breadcrumbs.

When the dumplings are cooked, roll them in the breadcrumbs, then sprinkle with the remaining cinnamon sugar.

EATING OUT

Czech towns and cities have many different types of eating places, with the greatest range of cuisines found in Prague. Czechs love to eat out and do so whenever their budget allows. A visiting friend is reason enough to have dinner at a popular restaurant or to step out for a beer at the pub.

In Prague, there are more than 1,300 pubs, some of which were established centuries ago. The historic pubs are now tourist haunts. Pubs serve food as well as beer, some of them running to roasts, goulash, sauerkraut—and of course dumplings. Wine bars usually sell snacks as well, and some serve full meals. The wines found in most bars are from Czech or Slovakian wineries.

Czechs frequent the many simple, self-service, cafeteria-style places, often only stand-up, that offer soups and staples like dumplings, sandwiches, salads, sausages, and goulash at reasonable prices. In Prague, there is a tradition of elegant coffee houses that serve coffee as well as numerous other drinks, except beer, and a selection of snacks and pastries. Recent innovations are bookshops with cafés or restaurants attached. The Slovak-style rustic restaurant, which is found throughout the Czech Republic, typically serves barbecued chicken. Vegetarians have limited choices when dining out.

Eating and drinking are significant activities for Czechs, and the portions served in restaurants are generous. For good food and a convivial atmosphere, there is no better place to taste the traditions of the republic than in one of its numerous bars, cafés, or restaurants.

Eating out is expensive. Fortunately, Czechs enjoy picking from nature—for free—and bottling their harvest to add to their meals at home throughout the year.

A
B
C

GERMANY

1

POLAN

Mt. Sněžka
(5,258 ft/
1,602m)

*Sudeten
Mountains*

● Liberec

● Ústí nad
Labem

*Krkonoše Mts.
(Giant Mts.)*

● Most

● Chomutov

O r e   M t s.

Labe

● Jáchymov

● Terezín

● Chlum

● Hradec
Králové

Františkovy
Lázně
●

● Karlovy
Vary

Ohře

● Cheb

● PRAGUE

● Poděbrady

● Pardubice

● Mariánské
Lázně

● Kutná Hora

Berounka

2

● Plzeň

● Příbram

B O H E M I A

Vltava

● Tábor

Bohemian-Moravian

● Brno

Šumava Mts.

Bohemian Forest

● Temelín

Highlands

● Dukovany

● České
Budějovice
(Budweis) ●

*Lake
Rozmberk*

● Třeboň

Dyje

● Český
Krumlov ●

Vltava

● Mikulo

*Lipno
Dam*

GERMANY

AUSTRIA

3

CZECH REPUBLIC

D

N

Feet		Meters
16,500		5,000
9,900		3,000
6,600		2,000
3,300		1,000
1,650		500
660		200
0		0

- Capital city
- Major town
- ▲ Mountain peak

Silesia

Ostrava

Odra

Omouc

M O R A V I A

Javorníky Mts.

Zlín

Morava

Strážnice

White Carpathian Mountains

S L O V A K I A

| 0 | 20 | 40 | 60 Miles |
| 0 | 40 | | 80 Kilometers |

Austria, B3-C3

Berounka River, A2
Bohemia, A2-B2
Bohemian Forest, A2-A3
Bohemian-Moravian
  Highlands, B2-C2
Brno, C2

České Budějovice
  (Budweis), B3
Český Krumlov, B3
Cheb, A2
Chlum, C1
Chomutov, A1

Dukovany, C3
Dyje River, C3

Františkovy Lázně, A1

Germany, A1-A3

Hradec Králové, C1

Jáchymov, A1
Javorníky Mountains, D2
Jeseníky Mountains, C2

Karlovy Vary, A1
Krkonoše (Giant)
  Mountains, B1-C1
Kutná Hora, B2

Labe River, B1
Liberec, B1
Lipno Dam, B3

Mariánské Lázně, A2
Mikulov, C3

Morava River, C3-D2
Moravia, C2-D2
Most, A1

Odra River, D2
Ohre River, A1-A2
Olomouc, C2
Ore Mountains, A1
Ostrava, D2

Pardubice, C2
Plzeň, A2
Poděbrady, B2
Poland, C1
Prague, B2
Příbram, B2

Rožmberk, Lake, B3

Silesia, D2
Slovakia, D3
Sněžka, Mount, B1
Strážnice, C3
Sudeten Mountains, C1
Šumava Mountains, A2-A3

Tábor, B2
Temelín, B2
Terezín, B1
Třeboň, B3

Ústi nad Labem, B1

Vltava River, B2-B3

White Carpathian
  Mountains, D3

Zlín, D2

QUICK NOTES

OFFICIAL NAME
Czech Republic

GOVERNMENT
Parliamentary democracy

TOTAL AREA
30,379 square miles (78,703 square kilometers)

POPULATION
10,298,324 (1997 estimate)

POPULATION DENSITY
339 persons per square mile
(131 persons per square kilometer)
Population growth rate: –0.13%

CAPITAL
Prague

REGIONS
North Bohemia, West Bohemia, Central Bohemia, South Bohemia, East Bohemia, North Moravia, South Moravia, and Prague

NATIONAL COAT OF ARMS
In four parts—two parts with the Czech white twin-tailed crowned lion on a red background, one with the Moravian red and white checkered eagle on a blue background, and one with the Silesian black eagle on a gold background

NATIONAL FLAG
Two equal horizontal bands of white and red with a blue isosceles triangle on the hoist side

MAJOR RIVERS
Vltava (also called the Moldau), Labe (Elbe), Morava, and Odra (Oder)

MAJOR LAKE
Rožmberk

MAJOR DAM
Lipno

HIGHEST PEAK
Sněžka (5,258 ft/1,602 m)

OFFICIAL LANGUAGE
Czech

MAJOR RELIGION
Roman Catholicism

CURRENCY
Czech crown (koruna, Kc)
32.2 Kc = US$1

MAIN EXPORTS
Machinery and equipment, manufactured goods, raw materials and fuels, chemicals

NATURAL RESOURCES
Black and brown coal

LEADERS IN POLITICS
Tomáš Garrigue Masaryk, president 1918–35
Václav Havel, president since 1993
Václav Klaus, prime minister since 1992

GLOSSARY

Art Nouveau
Art style of the late 19th and early 20th centuries.

babička ("BAB-ish-ka")
Grandmother.

Bohemia
Geographical region in western Czech Republic.

Bohemian crystal
A famous type of crystal that has been cut in Bohemia for centuries.

Hapsburg
Austrian-German dynasty that ruled the Czech lands from 1526 until 1914.

Hradčany
The castle and its environs in Prague.

Hussite movement/Hussites
Religious movement named after the theologian and reformer Jan Hus (1369?–1415), whose followers were called Hussites.

knedliky ("KNED-liki")
Sweet or savory dumplings made from either a bread or potato base.

Moravia
Geographical region in eastern Czech Republic.

national revival movement
Czech nationalist movement in the late 18th and early 19th centuries, which saw the growth Czech literature, music, theater, and language.

Pan, Paní, Slečna
("PAHN," "PA-ni," "SLE-tchna")
Mister, Missus, Miss—forms of address.

Prague Spring
A period in the 1960s under President Alexander Dubček when civil liberties were greater than was usual under the communist regime.

Přemysl ("PRZHE-mysl")
A dynasty founded by and named after a peasant, who ruled Bohemia in the 9th century.

sauerkraut ("sour-krout")
Sweet-sour pickled cabbage, a common dish that shows the German influence.

Silesia
Historical region found in northeastern Czech Republic, as well as in Poland and Germany.

skansen **("SKAN-suhn")**
A Swedish term for an open-air museum of traditional architecture and furnishings.

Sokol
Mass exercise with banners and ribbons, enjoyed by thousands of Czechs at rallies.

Strážnice ("STRAJ-nitse")
The name of a town that hosts an International Folklore Festival.

Sudetenland
Northwestern region of Bohemia adjoining Germany.

BIBLIOGRAPHY

Haviland, Virginia. *Favorite Fairy Tales Told in Czechoslovakia*. New York: Beech Tree Books, 1995.

Holy, Ladislav. *The Little Czech and the Great Czech Nation*. Cambridge, England: Cambridge University Press, 1996.

Humphreys, Rob. *Czech Republic*. Hove, East Sussex: Wayland, 1997.

Nollen, Tim. *Culture Shock! Czech Republic*. Oregon: Graphic Arts, 1997.

Otfinoski, Steven. *The Czech Republic (Nations in Transition)*. New York: Facts On File, 1997.

Skilling, H. Gordon (editor). *Czechoslovakia 1918–1988*. London: Macmillan Academic & Professional Ltd., 1991.

Wheaton, Bernard & Zdenek Kavan. *The Velvet Revolution Czechoslovakia 1988–1991*. Colorado: Westview Press, Inc., 1992.

INDEX

INDEX

INDEX

PICTURE CREDITS